Graph-Based Methods for Natural Language Processing Workshop 2016 (TextGraphs-10)

Held at the 2016 Conference of the North American Chapter of the Association for Computational Linguistics: Human Language Technologies (NAACL HLT 2016)

San Diego, California, USA
17 June 2016

ISBN: 978-1-5108-2516-1

Printed from e-media with permission by:

Curran Associates, Inc.
57 Morehouse Lane
Red Hook, NY 12571

Some format issues inherent in the e-media version may also appear in this print version.

Printed by Curran Associates, Inc. (2016)

Association for Computational Linguistics
209 N. Eighth Street
Stroudsburg, Pennsylvania 18360

Phone: 1-570-476-8006
Fax: 1-570-476-0860

acl@aclweb.org

Additional copies of this publication are available from:

Curran Associates, Inc.
57 Morehouse Lane
Red Hook, NY 12571 USA
Phone: 845-758-0400
Fax: 845-758-2634
Email: curran@proceedings.com
Web: www.proceedings.com

TextGraphs-10

Graph-Based Methods for Natural Language Processing

Proceedings of the Workshop

June 17, 2016
San Diego, California, USA

Introduction to TextGraphs-10

Welcome to TextGraphs, the workshop on Graph-based Methods for Natural Language Processing. The tenth edition of the workshop is being organized on June 17, 2016, in conjunction with the 15th Annual Conference of the North American Chapter of the Association for Computational Linguistics: Human Language Technologies (NAACL-HLT), being held in San Diego, California, USA.

For the past ten years, the series of TextGraphs workshops has exposed and encouraged the synergy between the field of Graph Theory and Natural Language Processing (NLP). The mix between the two started small, with graph theoretical framework providing efficient and elegant solutions for NLP applications that focused on single documents for part-of-speech tagging, word sense disambiguation and semantic role labeling, got progressively larger with ontology learning and information extraction from large text collections, and has reached web scale through the new fields of research that focus on information propagation in social networks, rumor proliferation, e-reputation, multiple entity detection, language dynamics learning, and future events prediction to name a few.

The tenth edition of the TextGraphs workshop is the latest step in the series, focusing on issues and solutions for large-scale graphs, such as those derived for web-scale knowledge acquisition or social networks. This edition includes papers describing novel NLP problems and applications that have emerged in recent years, and are being tackled using novel graph-based methods and solutions. In this edition, we add a new focus area on the usage of graph-based methods and NLP techniques to connect to resources and applications in the Semantic Web, and present research works about graph-based methods in the field of Semantic Web that are associated with NLP related problems and applications. Bringing together researchers interested in Graph Theory applied to Natural Language Processing and Semantic Web, this workshop provides an environment for further integration of graph-based solutions into different research fields. We believe that this will lead to a deeper understanding of new theories of graph-based algorithms, create new approaches, and widen the usage of graphs.

We are lucky to have two excellent invited speakers for this year's event. We thank Eduard Hovy and Ivan Titov for their enthusiastic acceptance of our invitation. We also thank Graphiq for agreeing to sponsor a student registration and for accepting our invitation to demonstrate a practical application of graph-based methods for information retrieval and natural language processing tasks. Finally, we are thankful to the members of the program committee for their valuable and high quality reviews. All submissions have benefited from their expert feedback. Their timely contribution was the basis for accepting an excellent list of papers and making this edition of TextGraphs a success.

Tanmoy Chakraborty, Martin Riedl, and V.G.Vinod Vydiswaran
TextGraphs-10 Organizers
May 2016

Organizers:

Tanmoy Chakraborty, University of Maryland, USA
Martin Riedl, TU Darmstadt, Germany
V.G.Vinod Vydiswaran, University of Michigan, USA

Program Committee:

Sivaji Bandyopadhyay, Jadavpur University, Kolkata, India
Pushpak Bhattacharyya, IIT Bombay, India
Chris Biemann, TU Darmstadt, Germany
Asif Ekbar, Indian Institute of Technology, Patna, India
Filip Ginter, University of Turku, Finland
Michael Glass, IBM T. J. Watson Research, USA
Nanda Kambhatla, IBM Research, India
Roman Klinger, University Stuttgart, Germany
Shervin Malmasi, Harvard Medical School, USA
Gabor Melli, VigLink, USA
Rada Mihalcea, University of Michigan, USA
Alessandro Moschitti, University Trento, Italy
Animesh Mukherjee, IIT Kharagpur, India
Philippe Muller, Paul Sabatier University, France
Preslav Nakov, Qatar Foundation, Qatar
Günter Neumann, DFKI, Saarbrücken, Germany
Arzucan Özgür, Bogazici University, Turkey
Sebastian Pado, Stuttgart University
Alexander Panchenko, TU Darmstadt, Germany
Simone Paolo Ponzetto, Universität Mannheim, Germany
Stephan Roller, Unversity of Texas at Austin, USA
Shourya Roy, Xerox Research, India
Anders Søgaard, University of Copenhagen, Denmark
Amarnag Subramanya, Google, USA
Partha Pratim Talukdar, Indian Institute of Science, Bangalore, India
Aline Villavicencio, Federal University of Rio Grande do Sul, Brazil
Piek Vossen, University Amsterdam, Netherlands
Fabio Massimo Zanzotto, University of Rome, Italy

Invited Speaker and Demo Presentation:

Eduard Hovy, Carnegie Mellon University, USA
Ivan Titov, Universiteit van Amsterdam, Netherlands
Graphiq, USA

Table of Contents

Workshop Program

June 17, 2016

9:00–9:15	***Introduction***
9:15–10:15	*Invited Talk: Inducing Semantic Representations* Ivan Titov
10:15–10:30	*Embedding Senses for Efficient Graph-based Word Sense Disambiguation* Luis Nieto Piña and Richard Johansson
10:30–11:00	***Coffee Break***
11:00–11:25	*Context Tailoring for Text Normalization* Seniz Demir
11:25–11:40	*Cross-Lingual Question Answering Using Common Semantic Space* Amir Pouran Ben Veyseh
11:40–12:05	*Network Motifs May Improve Quality Assessment of Text Documents* Thomas Arnold and Karsten Weihe
12:05–12:20	*Better Together: Combining Language and Social Interactions into a Shared Representation* Yi-Yu Lai, Chang Li, Dan Goldwasser and Jennifer Neville
12:20–12:40	*Invited Demo: General purpose semantic platform as an information retrieval system* Graphiq
12:40–14:00	***Lunch***
14:00–14:15	*Visualization of Dynamic Reference Graphs* Ivan Rodin, Ekaterina Chernyak, Mikhail Dubov and Boris Mirkin
14:15–15:15	*Invited Talk: To be finalized* Eduard Hovy
15:15–15:30	***Conclusion***

June 17, 2016 (continued)

Embedding Senses for Efficient Graph-based Word Sense Disambiguation

Luis Nieto Piña and **Richard Johansson**
University of Gothenburg, Sweden
{luis.nieto.pina, richard.johansson}@gu.se

Abstract

We propose a simple graph-based method for word sense disambiguation (WSD) where sense and context embeddings are constructed by applying the Skip-gram method to random walks over the sense graph. We used this method to build a WSD system for Swedish using the SALDO lexicon, and evaluated it on six different annotated test sets. In all cases, our system was several orders of magnitude faster than a state-of-the-art PageRank-based system, while outperforming a random baseline soundly.

1 Introduction

Word sense disambiguation (WSD) is a difficult task for automatic systems (Navigli, 2009). The most accurate WSD systems build on supervised learning models trained on annotated corpora (Taghipour and Ng, 2015), but because of the difficulty of the sense annotation task (Artstein and Poesio, 2008), the luxury of supervised training is available for a few languages only.

An approach that circumvents the lack of annotated corpora is to take advantage of the information available in lexical knowledge bases (LKBs) like WordNet (Miller, 1995; Fellbaum, 1998). This kind of resource encodes word sense lexicons as graphs connecting lexically and semantically related concepts. Several methods are available that use LKBs for WSD (Navigli and Lapata, 2007; Agirre and Soroa, 2009). These approaches usually apply a relatively complex analysis of the underlying graph based on the context of a target word to disambiguate it; e.g., Agirre and Soroa (2009) use the Personalized PageRank algorithm to perform walks on the graph. However, these methods are computationally very costly, which makes them practically useless for large corpora.

In this paper, we investigate a more time-efficient approach to graph-based WSD. We represent the concepts in the LKB by training vector space models on synthetic datasets created using random walks on the LKB's graph. These synthetic datasets are built on the assumption that a random walk starting at a given node in the graph will be composed of interrelated concepts, effectively building a context for it. Training a vector space model on a collection of such data generated for each node in an LKB's graph would result in related concepts being represented near each other in the vector space, according to the distributional hypothesis (Harris, 1954). We then use these representations to perform context-based disambiguation taking advantage of the geometric notions of similarity typical of vector space models. Using simple mechanisms for disambiguation and random walks allows our method to be orders of magnitude faster while keeping its accuracy well above the random-sense baseline.

2 Model

2.1 Word sense vector space model

The Skip-gram model (Mikolov et al., 2013) is a neural network language model (Bengio et al., 2003) intended to produce high-quality word vector representations trained on large collections of text. In its original formulation these representations are limited to a vocabulary of word-forms extracted from the corpus used to train the model. The representations are dense vectors in a high-dimensional space in which it is expected that words with a similar meaning are represented near each other, which allows to associate a similarity measure with a geometrical distance measure. These representations are trained to, given a word, predict its context; the training algorithm, thus, works with two separate vector spaces in which context and target words are represented.

Proceedings of the 2016 Workshop on Graph-based Methods for Natural Language Processing, NAACL-HLT 2016, pages 1–5,
San Diego, California, June 17, 2016.

Skip-gram introduced a highly efficient approach to language modeling using a shallow neural architecture, which has also been extended to handle word *sense* representation (Neelakantan et al., 2014; Chen et al., 2014; Johansson and Nieto Piña, 2015b; Nieto Piña and Johansson, 2015). Our aim in this paper is to build *graph-based* word sense embeddings and apply them to the task of WSD as follows: Given a sentence with an ambiguous word, we can then compare the representation of its context words with each of the ambiguous word's sense representations to decide which of them fits the context better.

For this purpose we use a modified version of the original Skip-gram implementation by Levy and Goldberg (2014), `word2vecf`, which specifies separate target and context vocabularies, making it possible to represent word senses as targets while keeping the context vocabulary restricted to word forms.

2.2 Random walks as contexts

Given a node in a graph G, a random walk generates a random sequence of interconnected nodes by selecting randomly from the edges of the current node at each step. The length of the random walk is controlled by a stop probability p_s. I.e., at each node visited in the walk, the probability of stopping is p_s; if the walk does not stop, one of the node's edges is followed to include another node in the walk. We repeat this process a number of times N_{walk} for each node in G to obtain $|G| \times N_{\text{walk}}$ random walks, where $|G|$ is the number of nodes in G.

The nodes in G are expected to represent word senses, while its edges connect semantically related word senses. Thus, a sequence of nodes generated by a random walk is a set of related word senses. Our assumption is that such a sequence can be considered a context of its starting node: a set of words that are related to, and can appear together in real texts with, the word sense represented by that node, thus emulating real text sentences; to what extent this assumption holds depends of course on the structure of the LKB we are using. Previous efforts in building word embeddings have shown the plausibility of this approach (Goikoetxea et al., 2015).

It can also be argued that different senses of a word appear in different contexts (e.g., it is plausible that the *music* sense of *rock* appears together with *play* and *concert*, while not so much with *mineral* or *throw*). By generating contexts semantically related to a given sense of a word, we expect the resulting vectors trained on them to be effective in the task of word sense disambiguation. At the same time, as the same number of contexts (random walks) are generated for each word sense (node in G), no word sense in the vocabulary contained in G is under-represented, as can be the case in real text corpora.

In order to conform to the definition of context vocabulary given above, given that nodes in G represent senses, those senses that form part of a context in a random walk will have to be mapped to their word-forms using a dictionary.

2.3 WSD mechanism

Given an ambiguous target word w_i in context $c_{i,j}$, $j = 1, \ldots, n$, our disambiguation mechanism assigns a score to each of its senses $s_{i,k}$, $k = 1, \ldots, K$, based on the dot product of the sense vector $v(s_{i,k})$ with the sum of the context vectors $v(c_{i,j})$:

$$v(s_{i,k})^{\mathsf{T}} \cdot \sum_{j=1}^{n} v(c_{i,j}) \qquad (1)$$

Note that all the information used to disambiguate originates from the LKB in the form of co-occurrence of concepts in RWs on the graph; no *external* information, like *a priori* sense probabilities, are used. The scores in Equation 1 are derived from the probability of the context words given a sense, calculated using the softmax function:

$$p(c_{i,1}, \ldots, c_{i,n} | s_{i,k}) = \frac{e^{v(s_{i,k})^{\mathsf{T}} \cdot \sum_{j=1}^{n} v(c_{i,j})}}{\sum_{k'=1}^{K} e^{v(s_{i,k'})^{\mathsf{T}} \cdot \sum_{j=1}^{n} v(c_{i,j})}}.$$

This expression is based on Skip-gram's objective function used to maximize the probability of a context given a target word. In our method, then, each ambiguous word is disambiguated by maximizing its sense scores (Eq. 1) and selecting the highest scoring sense for that instance.

3 Experiments

We built a WSD system for Swedish by applying the random walk-based training described above to the SALDO lexicon (Borin et al., 2013). In the experiments, we then evaluated this system on six different annotated corpora, in which the ambiguous words have been manually disambiguated according to SALDO, and compared it to random and first-sense baselines and UKB (Agirre and Soroa, 2009), a state-of-the-art graph-based WSD system.

3.1 The SALDO Lexicon

SALDO is the largest freely available lexical resource of this kind available for Swedish: the version used in this paper contains roughly 125,000 entries organized into a single semantic network. Similarly to WordNet (Fellbaum, 1998), SALDO is a large, manually constructed, and general-purpose lexicon that defines the senses in terms of a semantic network. But there are also important differences between WordNet and SALDO, first of all that the sense distinctions in SALDO tend to be more coarse-grained than in WordNet.

The SALDO network is defined in terms of semantic *descriptors*. A descriptor of a sense is another sense used to define its meaning. The most important descriptor is called the *primary* descriptor (PD), and since every sense in SALDO (except an abstract root sense) has a unique PD, the PD subgraph of SALDO forms a tree. A sense can be related to its primary descriptor through hyponymy, synonymy, meronym, antonymy, or some other relationship such as a predicate–argument relationship; this is another contrast with WordNet, where it is the hyponymy subgraph that forms the backbone. In practice, most PDs in SALDO are either synonyms or hypernyms.

To exemplify, Figure 3.1 shows a fragment of the PD tree. In the example, there are some cases where the senses are connected through hyponymy, such as *hard rock* being a type of *rock music*, but there are also other types of relations, such as *to play* being defined in terms of *music*.

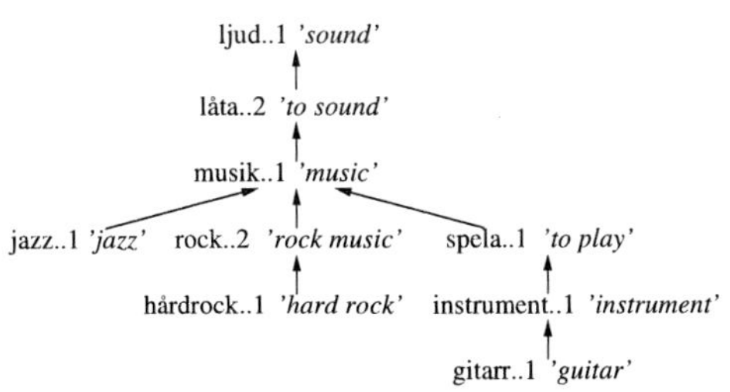

Figure 1: A part of the primary descriptor tree in SALDO.

In this work, we use the PD tree to generate the random walks. For instance, a random walk starting at *rock music* might consist of the senses corresponding to *music, play, instrument, guitar*. As mentioned above, these senses are then mapped back to their corresponding lemmas before being used as context features in `word2vecf`.

3.2 Evaluation Corpora

For development and evaluation, we used six different collections of sense-annotated examples. The first two, the *SALDO examples* (SALDO-ex) and *Swedish FrameNet examples* (SweFN-ex) consist of sentences selected by lexicographers to exemplify the senses (Johansson and Nieto Piña, 2015a). The former is dominated by the most frequent verbs, while the latter has a more even distribution. In our experiments, these two collections were used as a development set to tune the system's parameters.

The additional four collections are taken from an ongoing annotation project (Johansson et al., 2016); each collection corresponds to a domain: blogs, novels, Wikipedia, and Europarl (Koehn, 2005). Unlike the two collections mentioned above, in which the instances have been selected by lexicographers to be prototypical and to have a good coverage of the sense variation, the instances in these four collections are sampled uniformly from running text.

Corpus	Size	$\bar{n}_s$
SALDO-ex	1055	3.1
SweFN-ex	1309	2.9
Blogs	1014	2.9
Europarl	1282	2.7
Novels	1204	3.0
Wikipedia	1311	2.7

Table 1: Evaluation corpus statistics.

We preprocessed the examples in the six collections to tokenize, compound-split, and lemmatize the texts, and to determine the set of possible senses in a given context. We used content words only: nouns, verbs, adjectives, and adverbs. All unambiguous instances were removed from the sets, and we also excluded sentences where the target was a multiword expression or a part of a compound word. We also removed a few instances that could not be lemmatized unambiguously.[1] Table 1 shows the number of instances in each collection, as well as the average number of senses per instance ($\bar{n}_s$).

[1]Note that this is done only to facilitate comparison to the UKB model; it is not necessary for our system.

3.3 Evaluation

A model is trained on synthetic datasets compiled from random walks on SALDO. These walks are parameterized by their stop probability p_{stop}, which effectively controls the length of the random walk and has two effects: it impacts the size of training data (a lower p_{stop} will generate longer walks on average, and vice versa); and it controls the level of relatedness between the target sense and the words included in the context—a longer walk will wander away from the initial sense, including increasingly unrelated concepts, while a shorter one will keep its concepts closely related.

We tuned the model by training several versions with different p_{stop} and evaluated their performance on the development datasets. As the best-performing parameterization, we chose $p_{\text{stop}} = 0.25$, which generates random walks with an average length of 3.75 nodes and achieves an accuracy of 51.6% on the development datasets. In all cases, the vector space's dimensionality for senses and contexts is 200, and 10 iterations of the training algorithm are used.

Using this parameterization, we trained models on two different RW datasets: on one, random walks were performed on an unweighted version of SALDO (i.e., all edges are equally probable from any given node); on the other, the graph was weighted favoring the selection of a node's unique PD, with probability 0.5, over inverse (incoming) PD connections, which were uniformly distributed over the remaining probability mass.

The disambiguation mechanism explained in Section 2 is applied to sentences containing one ambiguous word using the sense and context representations that result from training the models: A score is calculated for each of the senses of an ambiguous target word in a context window of size 10 (to each side of the target word) and the highest scoring sense is selected to disambiguate the entry. The accuracy of the method is then obtained by comparing these selections with the annotations of the test datasets.

The results of evaluating this models on each component of the test dataset are shown in Table 2. The performance of the UKB model[2] by Agirre and Soroa (2009) on our datasets is also shown in this table, along with first-sense (S1) and random-sense baselines (Rand). These figures show that the first-sense approach is still a hard baseline. Amongst our two models (RW), the one trained on a weighted graph (w) performs consistently better; both of them outperform by a wide margin the random-sense baseline. The accuracy on the development sets is generally lower, especially in the case of the first-sense baseline, underlying their difference in nature with respect to the test sets (see Section 3.2).

Corpus	RW (uw)	RW (w)	UKB	S1	Rand
SALDO-ex	52.1	51.6	55.5	53.2	39.3
SweFN-ex	51.0	49.5	53.7	54.3	40.3
Blogs	49.8	58.0	70.0	72.4	40.8
Europarl	55.7	59.4	67.6	67.9	42.3
Novels	56.6	59.9	70.1	77.2	40.1
Wikipedia	60.4	59.6	69.5	76.8	41.2

Table 2: WSD accuracies on the development and test sets.

Regarding execution times, the tested models take a few hours to train and, once trained, are able to disambiguate over 8 000 instances per second, significantly surpassing the UKB model's times, which disambiguates approximately 8 instances per second. This is related to the fact that the complexity of our disambiguation mechanism is linear on the context vectors (see Equation 1), while the UKB model's is dependent on the graph size.

4 Conclusion

In this paper we have presented a WSD method trained on a synthetic corpus composed of random walks over an LKB's graph. This method has been shown to be very efficient, disambiguating thousands of words per second. While the accuracy obtained by the method does not beat that of comparable approaches, it is several orders of magnitude faster while outperforming a random-sense baseline. As has been shown in the results, the way in which random walks are generated seems to have an influence on the results; exploring alternative ways of generating training datasets might be a way of improving the model's results while retaining its efficiency.

Acknowledgments

This research was funded by the Swedish Research Council under grant 2013–4944.

[2]We used version 2.0 of UKB, run in the *word-by-word* mode, using an unweighted graph based on the PD tree.

References

Eneko Agirre and Aitor Soroa. 2009. Personalizing PageRank for word sense disambiguation. In *Proceedings of the 12th Conference of the European Chapter of the Association for Computational Linguistics*, pages 33–41. Association for Computational Linguistics.

Ron Artstein and Massimo Poesio. 2008. Inter-coder agreement for computational linguistics. *Computational Linguistics*, 34(4):555–596.

Yoshua Bengio, Réjean Ducharme, Pascal Vincent, and Christian Jauvin. 2003. A neural probabilistic language model. *Journal of Machine Learning Research*, 3:1137–1155.

Lars Borin, Markus Forsberg, and Lennart Lönngren. 2013. SALDO: a touch of yin to WordNet's yang. *Language Resources and Evaluation*, 47:1191–1211.

Xinxiong Chen, Zhiyuan Liu, and Maosong Sun. 2014. A unified model for word sense representation and disambiguation. In *Proceedings of the 2014 Conference on Empirical Methods in Natural Language Processing (EMNLP)*, pages 1025–1035.

Christiane Fellbaum, editor. 1998. *WordNet: An electronic lexical database*. MIT Press.

Josu Goikoetxea, Aitor Soroa, and Eneko Agirre. 2015. Random walks and neural network language models on knowledge bases. In *Proceedings of the 2015 Conference of the North American Chapter of the Association for Computational Linguistics: Human Language Technologies*, pages 1434–1439, Denver, Colorado, May–June. Association for Computational Linguistics.

Zellig S Harris. 1954. Distributional structure. *Word*, 10(2-3):146–162.

Richard Johansson and Luis Nieto Piña. 2015a. Combining relational and distributional knowledge for word sense disambiguation. In *Proceedings of the 20th Nordic Conference of Computational Linguistics*, pages 69–78, Vilnius, Lithuania.

Richard Johansson and Luis Nieto Piña. 2015b. Embedding a semantic network in a word space. In *Proceedings of the 2015 Conference of the North American Chapter of the Association for Computational Linguistics: Human Language Technologies*, pages 1428–1433, Denver, Colorado, May–June. Association for Computational Linguistics.

Richard Johansson, Yvonne Adesam, Gerlof Bouma, and Karin Hedberg. 2016. A multi-domain corpus of Swedish word sense annotation. In *Proceedings of the Language Resources and Evaluation Conference (LREC)*, Portorož, Slovenia.

Phillip Koehn. 2005. Europarl: A parallel corpus for statistical machine translation. In *MT summit*, pages 79–86.

Omer Levy and Yoav Goldberg. 2014. Dependency-based word embeddings. In *Proceedings of the 52nd Annual Meeting of the Association for Computational Linguistics*, volume 2, pages 302–308, Baltimore, Maryland, June. Association for Computational Linguistics.

Tomas Mikolov, Ilya Sutskever, Kai Chen, Greg S Corrado, and Jeff Dean. 2013. Distributed representations of words and phrases and their compositionality. In *Advances in Neural Information Processing Systems*, pages 3111–3119.

George A Miller. 1995. WordNet: a lexical database for English. *Communications of the ACM*, 38(11):39–41.

Roberto Navigli and Mirella Lapata. 2007. Graph connectivity measures for unsupervised word sense disambiguation. In *IJCAI*, pages 1683–1688.

Roberto Navigli. 2009. Word sense disambiguation: A survey. *ACM Comput. Surv.*, 41(2):10:1–10:69, February.

Arvind Neelakantan, Jeevan Shankar, Alexandre Passos, and Andrew McCallum. 2014. Efficient non-parametric estimation of multiple embeddings per word in vector space. In *Proceedings of the 2014 Conference on Empirical Methods in Natural Language Processing (EMNLP)*, pages 1059–1069, Doha, Qatar, October. Association for Computational Linguistics.

Luis Nieto Piña and Richard Johansson. 2015. A simple and efficient method to generate word sense representations. In *Proceedings of the International Conference Recent Advances in Natural Language Processing*, pages 465–472, Hissar, Bulgaria, September.

Kaveh Taghipour and Hwee Tou Ng. 2015. One million sense-tagged instances for word sense disambiguation and induction. In *Proceedings of the Nineteenth Conference on Computational Natural Language Learning*, pages 338–344, Beijing, China, July. Association for Computational Linguistics.

Context Tailoring for Text Normalization

Seniz Demir
TUBITAK BILGEM
Kocaeli, TURKEY
seniz.demir@tubitak.gov.tr

Abstract

Language processing tools suffer from significant performance drops in social media domain due to its continuously evolving language. Transforming non-standard words into their standard forms has been studied as a step towards proper processing of ill-formed texts. This work describes a normalization system that considers contextual and lexical similarities between standard and non-standard words for removing noise in texts. A bipartite graph that represents contexts shared by words in a large unlabeled text corpus is utilized for exploring normalization candidates via random walks. Input context of a non-standard word in a given sentence is tailored in cases where a direct match to shared contexts is not possible. The performance of the system was evaluated on Turkish social media texts.

1 Introduction

Social media has been an integral part of personal communication in the last decade. Everyday, people willingly produce millions of multilingual texts since they are free in the way how they express themselves. Grammatical rules and language structures do not have to be all in place, even the words might not be properly written. However, free-style writing and ever-growing nature of the language hinder the utility of social media texts in computational linguistics studies. For instance, non-standard words (e.g.,"comin soon" for "coming soon") and phonetic substitutions (e.g., "4u" for "for you") that are often seen in social media texts degrade the performance of many NLP tools such as parsers and named entity recognizers (Foster et al., 2011; Kucuk and Steinberger, 2014). Being trained on formal texts is the major drawback of these tools in processing ill-formed texts. In addition, different social media genres have their own characteristics and various factors (e.g., demographic background and age) trigger linguistic changes in social media language over time (Eisenstein et al., 2014; Herdagdelen, 2013; Schwartz et al., 2013).

Normalizing ill-formed texts is a promising preprocessing step to address experienced accuracy drops in existing NLP tools. This paper proposes a normalization system that transforms non-standard out of vocabulary (OOV) words into their standard in vocabulary (IV) forms. We argue that contextual and lexical characteristics of words are of the greatest importance in normalization. To encode contextual similarities of words, a bipartite graph acquired from a corpus of formal and informal texts is utilized. The first bipartite of the graph consists of words that appear in the contexts represented by the second bipartite. This graphical representation not only captures the way how words are used in real texts but also presents lexical variants of the same word in similar contexts.

A non-standard word might be restored to different words depending on its context in a sentence. In this work, one consideration that is exploited in determining the right form of a non-standard word is its input context and the similarity of this context to other contexts captured by the underlying graph. At the core of our normalization system lies a novel use of a tailoring approach on input contexts. Tailored input contexts are shown to be effective in finding

Proceedings of the 2016 Workshop on Graph-based Methods for Natural Language Processing, NAACL-HLT 2016, pages 6–14,
San Diego, California, June 17, 2016. ©2016 Association for Computational Linguistics

similar contexts in the graph. To normalize a non-standard word, our system determines contextually similar candidate normalizations by performing random walks through similar contexts. Additional normalization candidates are extracted from a word lexicon by measuring their lexical distances to the ill-formed word via a well-known similarity metric. We evaluated our normalization system on 715 Turkish social media sentences with 1190 ill-formed words in total and our promising results revealed that we improve on state-of-the-art in Turkish.

2 Related Work

Text normalization has been extensively studied in the literature. Noisy channel model where posterior probabilities are used to find the most probable form of a non-standard word has pioneered normalization research (Brill and Moore, 2000; Tautanova and Moore, 2002; Choudhury et al., 2007; Cook and Stevenson, 2009). Handling the transformation in normalization as a translation from an ill-formed text to a formal text has also been experimented (Aw et al., 2006; Kaufmann and Kalita, 2010). These earlier studies have relied on hand annotated data and proper categorization of non-standard words.

A recent work has used a letter transformation approach where the generation of a non-standard word from a standard word is modeled at the character level. Visual priming and string/phonetic similarity have also been incorporated into the transformation model (Liu et al., 2011; Liu et al., 2012). Generating a confusion set of in-vocabulary word candidates for an out-of-vocabulary word and selecting the best candidate according to lexical string similarity and contextual features have been studied (Han et al., 2013). More recently, distributed word representations (Kumar and Sridhar, 2015) and recurrent neural networks (Chrupala, 2014) have been used to address the normalization problem.

Our work is closely related to the latter line of research which has used graphical representations to capture contextual similarities between words. The work of Sönmez and Özgür (2014) has addressed the normalization problem via a word-association graph where the graph represents POS tags of words and their relative positions to each other in written texts. The proposed approach has achieved a 94.1% precision on a shared English dataset by taking contextual, grammatical, and lexical features of words into account. Our work differs from their approach in several aspects. First, we take into account all words in the input context of an ill-formed word at once (if possible) rather than aggregating individual relations of an ill-formed word with each word in its context. Second, we do not benefit from the part-of-speech of an ill-formed word during normalization but it plays an important role in their unsupervised approach. In another approach, the underlying graph has been used to assess how contextually similar two words are (Hassan and Menezes, 2013). Randomly traversing the graph, a normalization lexicon was induced and later used to generate word confusion sets of non-standard words. This work, which generates the same confusion set for an OOV word in different input contexts, has achieved a precision of 92.43% on English social media texts.

Unfortunately, a few recent studies have focused on text normalization in Turkish. In the cascaded approach (Torunoğlu and Eryiğit, 2014), seven different transformations (e.g., vowel restoration and accent normalization) have been developed to restore OOV words to their IV word forms. The approach has achieved an accuracy of 71% on a set of 600 Turkish tweets. The most recent model (Yıldırım and Yıldız, 2015) has utilized a variety of techniques (e.g., lexical similarity and language model based contextual similarity) to handle different normalization problems and a precision of 80% has been reported on Turkish tweets.

3 Normalization Equivalences

We argue that an ill-formed word and its standard rendering (normalization equivalence) have some characteristics that should be considered in normalization. First, a standard word replaces its ill-formed version in any sentence without a loss in meaning. Therefore, shared contexts where standard and non-standard words both appear give important clues for normalization. Second, transformation from an ill-formed word to different standard words is possible. For instance, the word 'aaba' in the sentence "aaba annem de okulumu sevecek mi?"{I wonder if my mother will also like my school?} should be normalized as 'acaba'{I wonder}. However, that word should be normalized as 'araba'{car} in the sentence "aaba sürmek benim için büyük keyif"{Driving car is a great pleasure for me.}. Thus, input context of an ill-formed word is of great importance and cannot be ignored in normalization. Third, character-based edit operations (i.e, insertion, deletion, or substitution) produce non-standard forms of a word. These operations might be phonetic, graphemic, typographic, etc. (Liu et al., 2012). For instance, the ill-formed word 'ailelerne' can be produced from standard words 'ailelere' (with one insertion) and 'ailelerine' (with one deletion). Therefore, ill-formed words and their standard forms are lexically/phonetically similar.

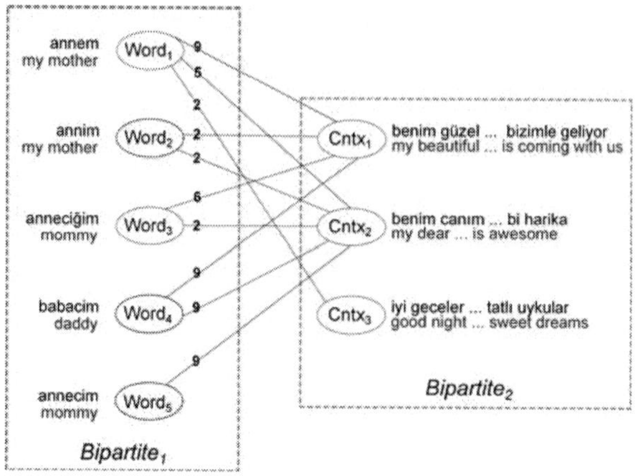

Figure 1: A bipartite graph built from a set of word sequences.

3.1 Shared Contexts

We treat the context of a word as an n-gram word sequence that has the word at its center. For instance, consider the 5-gram word sequence $w_1w_2w_3w_4w_5$. Here, the context of the word w_3 consists of the two words on its left and the two words on its right $w_1w_2w_4w_5$. Our system uses a bipartite graph to represent words and their contexts. The first bipartite contains words **(word nodes)** and the second bipartite represents contexts where these words appear **(context nodes)**. A word node is connected to a context node with an undirected edge if the word appears in that context. For instance, Figure 1 shows a bipartite graph[1] constructed from a set of 5-gram sequences where an edge weight represents co-occurrence count of the corresponding word and context in the set. A context node might be connected to more than one word node. We refer to these context nodes as "shared contexts" such as the nodes Cntx_1 and Cntx_2 in Figure 1.

3.2 Context of an Ill-Formed Word

The input context of an ill-formed word is also represented as an n-gram word sequence. In our system, two kinds of contexts are used for an ill-formed word. The central context is an n-gram sequence which has the ill-formed word at its center. However, sliding contexts are those n-gram sequences which have the ill-formed word at any position but the center. An ill-formed word might have an incomplete central context with one or more missing words ($\emptyset^2$) due to its position in a sentence. One or more sliding contexts are always possible for an ill-formed word with/without missing words. For instance, consider the sentence "bugünn oğlumu gösterisi için hazırlıyıp fotoğraflarını çekeceğim"{Today, I will prepare my son for his show and take his photos}. The contexts extracted for the ill-formed words of the sentence using 5-gram sequences are shown below:

Word: **'bugünn'{today}**
Central context: [∅, ∅, oğlumu, gösterisi]
Sliding contexts: [bugünn, oğlumu, için, hazırlıyıp]

Word: **'hazırlıyıp'{prepare}**
Central context: [gösterisi, için, fotoğraflarını, çekeceğim]
Sliding contexts: [bugünn, oğlumu, için hazırlıyıp], [oğlumu, gösterisi, hazırlıyıp, fotoğraflarını]

3.3 Edit Operations

In our system, only one-to-one word normalizations where an ill-formed word is restored to a single standard word are considered. In such cases, a standard word represents a number of edit operations (e.g., insertion or substitution) once aligned to its ill-formed lexical variant at the character level. We capture the operations that a standard word experience using a well-known lexical similarity metric.

[1] The word nodes Word_2, Word_4, and Word_5 represent OOV words whereas nodes Word_1 and Word_3 represent IV words.

[2] The symbol ∅ refers to any word.

4 Normalization Approach

Once a sentence is given, our system analyzes all words using a morphological parser and those that cannot be parsed are accepted as OOV words. For each OOV word, normalization candidates which reflect all characteristics that we consider in this work are explored in the underlying graph. This exploration, performed by a number of random walks, can benefit from three pieces of information: the ill-formed word, its input contexts, and all kinds of information captured by the underlying graph. A word lexicon that consists of standard IV words is also examined to identify candidate normalizations that are lexically similar to the OOV word. Finally, one candidate is selected from among all candidates as the best normalization of the OOV word.

4.1 Contextual Similarity via Random Walks

A random walk starts from a node of a bipartite and consists of a number of sequential steps taken from one bipartite to another (from word node to context node and vice versa). A step cannot be taken within a bipartite since there are no connections between its nodes. Transition probabilities (TP) from the current node are used to determine which node(s) will be visited next.

$$\text{TP}_{ab} = \text{TFreq}^{1,2}_{ab} \;/\; \sum_{x \in Neighs(a)} \text{TFreq}^{1,2}_{ax}$$

$$\text{TFreq}^{1}_{ab} = \text{Weight}_{ab} \;/\; \text{Freq(b)}$$

$$\text{TFreq}^{2}_{ab} = \text{Weight}_{ab}$$

TFreq^{1}_{ab} measures the transition frequency from a context node (a) to a word node (b) and TFreq^{2}_{ab} measures the transition frequency from a word node (a) to a context node (b). Weight_{ab} corresponds to the weight of the edge connecting nodes a and b in the graph. Although moving to a common word is penalized by taking into account its frequency in the corpus (Freq(b)), no penalty is applied to contexts shared by many words.

In our system, the maximum number of steps that can be taken in a random walk is limited. A random walk ends when a word node representing a standard word is reached or the maximum number of steps is exhausted without reaching a standard word node. For instance, assume that the graph shown in Figure 1 is a subgraph of a larger bipartite graph where the word nodes have connections to other context nodes that are not shown in the graph. Assume also that two possible random walks of at most 4 steps from Word_2 are performed on the graph, which are Word_2-Cntx_1-Word_1 (with two steps) and Word_2-Cntx_1-Word_4-Cntx_2-Word_5 (with four steps). In this scenario, the first walk ends at Word_1 since it represents a standard word but the second walk ends at Word_5 since the maximum number of steps is taken without reaching a standard word node.

The node from where a random walk starts **(initial node)** is of great importance in a graph with so many nodes and connections due to the limited number of steps. Since these walks are for identifying candidate normalizations for an ill-formed word, all available information about that word should be utilized in selecting the initial node. It is straightforward to select the node representing ill-formed word as the initial node and to explore normalization candidates by randomly walking from this node. However, this approach would fail in utilizing other valuable information sources, namely input contexts of the word. We argue that input contexts of the ill-formed word should be used in determining the initial node and restricting the space of neighbor nodes to be visited from the initial node. Our approach uses similarities between the central context of the ill-formed word and contexts represented by the graph to determine the initial node.

Two contexts are treated as similar if they are exactly the same or a match can be achieved if any of them is tailored by compromising from its contextual content. A context can be tailored by relaxing constraints put by contained words. In determining the initial node, only central contexts are tailored by replacing one or more contained words with $\emptyset$ symbol, which in turn can match to any word. For instance, the context [yemek, yaparken, fazla, kullanmak]{using ... a lot while cooking} turns to be similar to the context [yemek, yaparken, az, kullanmak]{using ... a little while cooking} if it is tailored to [yemek, yaparken, $\emptyset$, kullanmak]. Relaxing restrictions enables more contexts to be explored in the underlying graph but makes central context less beneficiary for reducing randomness. For instance, consider the central context [Word_1, Word_2,

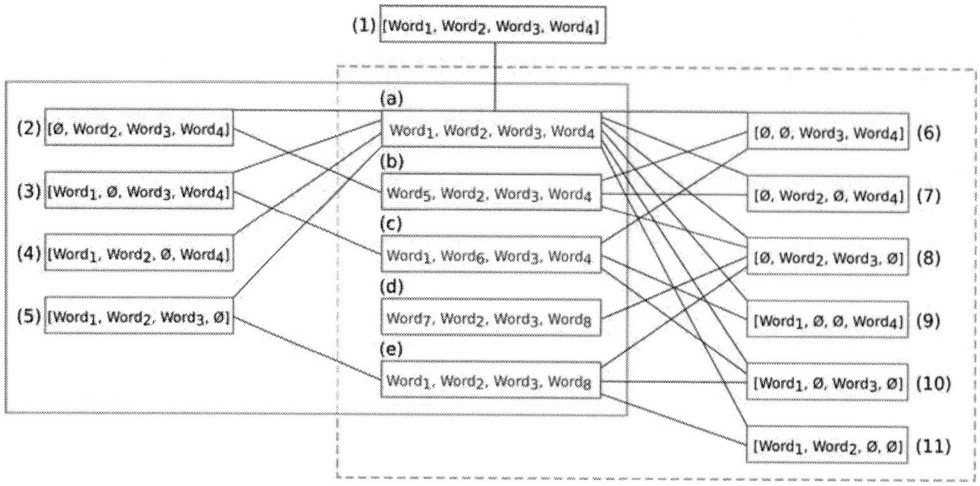

Figure 2: Context tailoring.

$Word_3$, $Word_4$] shown in Figure 2. This context directly matches Context (a) but not the Contexts (b) - (e). The central context can be tailored to Contexts (2), (3), (4), and (5) by relaxing restrictions put by a single word whereas to Contexts (6), (7), (8), (9), (10), and (11) with two words. The more restrictions are relaxed, the more similar contexts are found (e.g., Context (d)) in the underlying graph.

Our approach first identifies the node representing the ill-formed word and its neighbor context nodes. If any of these connected context nodes matches the central context of the word, it is identified as the initial node. If a direct match is not possible, the central context is tailored in turns until similar contexts are found among the neighbors. At each turn, all possible contexts obtained by relaxing the restriction put by a single word in tailored contexts of the previous turn are used. The neighbor nodes that represent contexts similar to a tailored form of the central context are identified as initial nodes. If a similar context is not found until the tailoring threshold is reached[3], the node that represents the ill-formed word is used as the initial node.

On the other hand, if the ill-formed word does not appear in the underlying graph, its central context is compared to all contexts represented in the graph using the same tailoring methodology. Context nodes that represent similar contexts to tailored central context are identified as initial nodes. If more than one initial node is identified, random walks could be performed either from one or some, or even all nodes depending on the traversal strategy. For instance, assume that an ill-formed word is connected to the Contexts (a) - (e) shown in Figure 2. Initial nodes determined for that word in some representative central contexts are shown below:

- Context: [$Word_1$, $Word_2$, $Word_7$, $Word_4$]
  Initial Node: Context (a)
- Context: [$Word_1$, $Word_2$, $Word_4$, $Word_9$]
  Initial Nodes: Context (a) & Context (e)

For an ill-formed word, a fixed number of random walks are performed starting from the same initial node(s) in order to find its normalization candidates. We treat a standard word where any random walk ends as contextually similar to the ill-formed word. For instance, after the walk $Word_2$-$Cntx_1$-$Word_1$ in Figure 1, the words 'annim' and 'annem' are considered as contextually similar.

4.2 Positional Similarity

An ill-formed word might not be represented as a word node in the underlying graph if it does not appear at the center of an n-gram word sequence. Nonetheless, its position in a context still provides insights into how that word could be normalized. In a nutshell, we search for other words that are rather used at the position of the ill-formed word in similar contexts. Here, sliding contexts of the ill-formed word are used. For each sliding context,

[3]We limit the number of $\emptyset$ symbols in a context.

the underlying graph is explored using the tailoring methodology in order to find similar contexts and to identify words that appear at the position of the ill-formed word in these contexts. We treat these words as positionally similar to the ill-formed word. For instance, assume that positionally similar words are searched for the word 'hazırlıyıp' in the sentence "bugünn oğlumu gösterisi için hazırlıyıp fotoğraflarını çekeceğim". Assume also that only the contexts shown below are identified as similar to the sliding contexts of that word (given in Section 3.2). In this scenario, positionally similar words to the word 'hazırlıyıp' are shown below in bold:

> [bugünn, oğlumu, için, **hazırlayıp**]
> [oğlumu, gösterisi, **süsleyip**, resimlerini]
> [oğlumu, gösterisi, **bezeyip**, fotoğraflarını]

4.3 Lexical Similarity

Lexical similarity of normalization equivalences is as important as their contextual similarity. For an ill-formed word, we also explore a lexicon of standard words as an external resource in order to determine lexically similar words among them. In this work, two well-known metrics, namely Longest Common Subsequence Ratio ($LCSR_{ab}$) and Edit Distance (ED_{ab}) are used to assess how lexically similar two words are (LexSim_{ab}):

$$\text{LexSim}_{ab} = \text{LCSR}_{ab} \;/\; \text{ED}_{ab}$$

$$\text{LCSR}_{ab} = \text{LCS}_{ab} \;/\; \text{Max}\langle \text{Length(a), Length(b)} \rangle$$

For instance, consider the ill-formed word 'köşlerine' which can be produced from a standard word 'köylerine'$\{$to their town$\}$ by substituting the 'y' character with 'ş' or from the word "köşelerine"$\{$to its corners$\}$ by dropping the 'e' character. Although the ill-formed word has the same edit distance to both words, its lexical similarity is 0.89 to 'köylerine' and 0.9 to 'köşelerine'.

4.4 Methodology

Our normalization methodology separately generates normalization candidates that are (i) contextually similar, (ii) positionally similar, and (iii) lexically similar to an ill-formed word. Contextually and positionally similar candidates whose edit distance to the ill-formed word is greater than a predetermined threshold are discarded. For each case, the remaining candidates are assigned a similarity score between 0 and 1. Contextual similarity score (CS_{ab}) is computed using the hitting time between two nodes (HT_{ab}). In this work, hitting time refers to the minimum number of steps taken to visit one node starting from the other node in any performed random walk[4]:

$$\text{CS}_{ab} = \text{Min}\langle \text{HT}_{ax} \rangle \;/\; \text{HT}_{ab}$$

Frequencies of contexts in the corpus on which the graph is built are used for computing positional similarity scores (PS_{ab}):

$$\text{PS}_{ab} = \text{Freq(Context}_b) \;/\; \text{Max}\langle \text{Freq(Context}_x) \rangle$$

Lexical similarity score (LS_{ab}) is computed using the LexSim formula:

$$\text{LS}_{ab} = \text{LexSim}_{ab} \;/\; \text{Max}\langle \text{LexSim}_{ax} \rangle$$

Finally, normalization scores of all candidates (NS_{ab}) are computed and the candidate with the highest score is selected as the normalized form of the ill-formed word[5]:

$$\text{NS}_{ab} = \lambda_1 \times \text{CS}_{ab} + \lambda_2 \times \text{PS}_{ab} + \lambda_3 \times \text{LS}_{ab}$$

5 Evaluation

In order to evaluate the performance of our language-independent system, we experimented with Turkish social media texts. For the study, we first collected a large corpus of noisy and clean Turkish texts from different resources. The corpus consisted of tweets (~11GB) that were retrieved via Twitter Streaming API from April to October 2015, 20 million publicly available tweets[6], and clean Turkish texts (~6GB). The corpus was preprocessed by first discarding non-Turkish content as identified

[4]Here, a refers to the ill-formed word, b refers to an IV word candidate, and x refers to any other candidate.

[5]Different strategies could be followed to compute normalization scores such as defining a precedence order over the kinds of similarities.

[6]http://www.kemik.yildiz.edu.tr/?id=28

by a language detection tool. Later, tweet-specific terms (e.g., # and RT), URLs, some punctuations, and repetitive characters were cleaned from the corpus. Finally, the remaining sentences of $\sim$9GB were tokenized into 7,401,321 distinct words.

We constructed a bipartite graph from the collected corpus using 5-gram word sequences. The word sequences contained one or more OOV words and in cases where there was only one OOV word, it might not be at the center. Statistics about the constructed graph is given in Table 1.

Bipartite	Number of Nodes	Average Degree	Average Edge Weight
Word	5,122,873	114.56	1.18
Context	567,078,012	1.03	

Table 1: Statistics about the graph.

In the study, if more than one initial node was determined for an ill-formed word, an equal number of random walks were performed from each of these nodes rather than selecting only one. 50 random walks with a maximum of 6 steps were performed from each initial node. Tailoring threshold was set to 1 for central contexts (a tailored context might have at most three $\emptyset$ symbols) whereas to 2 for sliding contexts. The edit distance threshold was set to 2 and contextually/positionally similar normalization candidates with a higher edit distance were discarded from consideration. Words were preprocessed before computing their edit distances. For instance, repetition of characters was reduced to a single character and words were deasciified to restore Turkish characters (if necessary). It is noteworthy to mention that our system do not normalize a word if an IV word candidate is not identified for that word.

Our test set consisted of 715 sentences that were retrieved from Twitter. The ill-formed words in these sentences were manually identified and normalized by two native Turkish speakers. 483 of these sentences contained only one ill-formed word. However, the remaining 232 sentences had at least two ill-formed words at different positions. Some sentences even had a number of ill-formed words in sequence. Our test set consisted of 1190 ill-formed words in total. Moreover, we observed different kinds of transformations between ill-formed words and their normalized forms (e.g., asciified Turkish characters, omitted characters, and typos).

As an example, consider one of our test sentences where ill-formed words are underlined "insanıar köprü kuracakıarı yerde duvar ördükıeri için yaınız kaıırıar"{People remain alone since they put up walls rather than building bridges}. The following shows how that sentence is normalized by a native speaker and by our system using different kinds of similarities:

Normalized Sentence: "insanlar köprü kuracakları yerde duvar ördükleri için yalnız kalırlar"
Contextual Similarity: "insanlar köprü kuracakları yerde duvar ördükleri için yalnız kalırlar
Positional Similarity: "insanıar köprü kuracakları yerde duvar ördükıeri için yaınız kaıırıar"
Lexical Similarity: "insanlar köprü kuracakları yerde duvar ördükleri için yalnız karar"

To our best knowledge, there is only one publicly available Turkish text normalization system (Torunoğlu and Eryiğit, 2014) that we can use in this evaluation in addition to a dictionary based MsWord spell checker. Neither the normalization system (TE_N) nor the spell checker (SP_C) utilizes the context of an OOV word during normalization. Table 2 shows the normalization results that we achieved on the whole test set along with the results of other normalizers. The third row (Con. Sim.) shows the performance of our system once only contextual similarities were considered during normalization ($\lambda_1 = 1, \lambda_2 = 0, \lambda_3 = 0$). Similarly, the fourth and fifth rows show the system's performance once positional and lexical similarities were considered respectively. The sixth row presents our baseline where all kinds of similarities had an equal effect on normalization ($\lambda_1 = 1, \lambda_2 = 1, \lambda_3 = 1$). The last row shows the results of our proposed system whose λ values were tuned on a development set of 200 sentences.

Normalizers	Precision	Recall	F-measure
SP_C	73.7%	71.5%	72.6%
TE_N	80.6%	77.3%	78.4%
Con. Sim.	73.6%	49.1%	58.9%
Pos. Sim.	88.1%	4.4%	8.3%
Lex. Sim.	86.1%	85.3%	85.7%
Con.+Pos.+Lex. Sim.	81.0%	80.3%	80.6%
Our System	**87.1%**	**86.3%**	**86.7%**

Table 2: Evaluation of all test sentences.

As shown in Table 2, a very low recall and the highest precision were obtained once the system considered only positional similarities between an OOV word and its IV word candidates. Moreover, our system achieved the highest F-measure and recall, and the second highest precision among all normalizers. Table 3 and Table 4 show the results obtained by our baseline and our system on sentences with only one OOV word and multiple OOV words respectively. Our system obtained higher scores in test sentences with multiple OOV words as compared to those with a single OOV word. This might be explained by the fact that a sentence written by the same person might contain multiple OOV words that underwent the same transformation (such as repetitive characters) which can be normalized by our system. On the other hand, several sentences might contain a single OOV word that experienced different kinds of transformations, some of which might not be handled by our system.

Normalizers	Precision	Recall	F-measure
Con.+Pos.+Lex. Sim.	79.3%	78.9%	79.1%
Our System	**81.9%**	**81.6%**	**81.8%**

Table 3: Evaluation of sentences with one OOV word.

Normalizers	Precision	Recall	F-measure
Con.+Pos.+Lex. Sim.	82.3%	81.3%	81.8%
Our System	**90.7%**	**89.7%**	**90.2%**

Table 4: Evaluation of sentences with multiple OOV words.

Overall, the evaluation results support our methodology for normalizing Turkish social media texts. It was our observation that replacing an OOV word with its normalized form before normalizing the next OOV word in the same sentence might end up with a totally different normalization. In the future, we will analyze the effects of such on-the-fly replacements on a large test set.

6 Conclusion

In this work, we describe a normalization system for social media texts. The system utilizes contextual and lexical similarities between non-standard and standard words for normalizing noisy texts. To encode contextual similarities, a bipartite graph is constructed from a large collection of texts where words and contexts that they appear in are connected with weighted edges. The graph is traversed via random walks in order to determine contextually similar normalization candidates for an ill-formed word. In determining the initial node(s) of these walks, input context of the ill-formed word is used either as is or after being tailored. An external word lexicon is used to explore normalization candidates that are lexically similar to the ill-formed word. The best candidate is selected based on its assigned similarity score. Our experiments on 715 Turkish tweets showed that our system achieved the state-of-the-art results. As future work, we plan to evaluate the system performance on other languages and to study how randomness in random walks can be reduced or totally eliminated to better gauge contextual similarities of words in real texts. Unfortunately, the morphological parser erroneously identifies some words (e.g., proper nouns) as OOV words and forces the system to treat these words as non-standard words. We will also study how this problem can be overcomed by using of other NLP tools such as named entity recognizers in the future.

References

AiTi Aw, Min Zhang, Juan Xiao, and Jian Su. 2006. A phrase-based statistical model for sms text normalization. In *Proceedings of the 21st International Conference on Computational Linguistics*, pages 33–40.

Eric Brill and Robert C. Moore. 2000. An improved error model for noisy channel spelling correction. In *Proceedings of the 38th Annual Meeting on Association for Computational Linguistics*, pages 286–293.

Çağıl Sönmez and Arzucan Özgür. 2014. A graph-based approach for contextual text normalization. In *Proceedings of the Conference on Empirical Methods on Natural Language Processing (EMNLP)*, pages 313–324.

Monojit Choudhury, Rahul Saraf, Vijit Jain, Animesh Mukherjee, Sudeshna Sarkar, and Anupam Basu. 2007. Investigation and modeling of the structure of texting language. *International Journal on Document Analysis and Recognition*, 10:157–174.

Grzegorz Chrupala. 2014. Normalizing tweets with edit scripts and recurrent neural embeddings. In *Proceedings of the 52nd Annual Meeting of the Association for Computational Linguistics*, pages 680–686.

Paul Cook and Suzanne Stevenson. 2009. An unsupervised model for text message normalization. In *Proceedings of the 4th Workshop on Computational Ap-*

proaches to Linguistic Creativity (CALC), pages 71–78.

Jacob Eisenstein, Brendan O'Connor, Noah A. Smith, and Eric P. Xing. 2014. Diffusion of lexical change in social media. *PLoS ONE*, 9:71–76.

Jennifer Foster, Özlem Çetinoğlu, Joachim Wagner, Joseph Le Roux, Stephen Hogan, Joakim Nivre, Deirdre Hogan, and Josef van Genabith. 2011. # hardtoparse: Pos tagging and parsing the twitterverse. In *Proceedings of the Workshop On Analyzing Microtext (AAAI)*, pages 20–25.

Bo Han, Paul Cook, and Timothy Baldwin. 2013. Lexical normalization for social media text. *ACM Transactions on Intelligent Systems and Technology (TIST)*, 4:1–27.

Hany Hassan and Arul Menezes. 2013. Social text normalization using contextual graph random walks. In *Proceedings of the 51st Annual Meeting of the Association for Computational Linguistics*, pages 1577–1586.

Amac Herdagdelen. 2013. Twitter n-gram corpus with demographic metadata. *Language Resources and Evaluation*, 47:1127–1147.

Max Kaufmann and Jugal Kalita. 2010. Syntactic normalization of twitter messages. In *Proceedings of the International conference on natural language processing*.

Dilek Kucuk and Ralf Steinberger. 2014. Experiments to improve named entity recognition on turkish tweets. In *Proceedings of the 5th Workshop on Language Analysis for Social Media*, pages 71–78.

Vivek Kumar and Rangarajan Sridhar. 2015. Unsupervised text normalization using distributed representations of words and phrases. In *Proceedings of the North American Chapter of the Association for Computational Linguistics: Human Language Technologies*, pages 8–16.

Fei Liu, Fuliang Weng, Bingqing Wang, and Yang Liu. 2011. Insertion, deletion, or substitution?: Normalizing text messages without pre-categorization nor supervision. In *Proceedings of the 49th Annual Meeting of the Association for Computational Linguistics: Human Language Technologies (HLT)*, pages 71–76.

Fei Liu, Fuliang Weng, and Xiao Jiang. 2012. A broad-coverage normalization system for social media language. In *Proceedings of the 50th Annual Meeting of the Association for Computational Linguistics*, pages 1035–1044.

H. Andrew Schwartz, Johannes C. Eichstaedt, Margaret L. Kern, Lukasz Dziurzynski, Stephanie M. Ramones, Megha Agrawal, Achal Shah, Michal Kosinski, David Stillwell, Martin E. P. Seligman, and Lyle H. Ungar. 2013. Personality, gender, and age in the language of social media: The open-vocabulary approach. *PLoS ONE*, 8.

Katia Tautanova and Robert C. Moore. 2002. A pronunciation modeling for improved spelling correction. In *Proceedings of the 40th Annual Meeting on Association for Computational Linguistics*, pages 144–151.

Dilara Torunoğlu and Gülşen Eryiğit. 2014. A cascaded approach for social media text normalization of turkish. In *Proceedings of the 5th Workshop on Language Analysis for Social Media (LASM)*, pages 62–70.

Savaş Yıldırım and Tuğba Yıldız. 2015. An unsupervised text normalization architecture for turkish language. In *16th International Conference on Intelligent Text Processing and Computational Linguistics (CICLING)*.

Cross-Lingual Question Answering Using Common Semantic Space

Amir Pouran Ben Veyseh
University of Tehran
Tehran, Iran
veyseh@ut.ac.ir

Abstract

With the advent of Big Data concept, a lot of attention has been paid to structuring and giving semantic to this data. Knowledge bases like DBPedia play an important role to achieve this goal. Question answering systems are common approach to address expressivity and usability of information extraction from knowledge bases. Recent researches focused only on monolingual QA systems while cross-lingual setting has still so many barriers. In this paper we introduce a new cross-lingual approach using a unified semantic space among languages. After keyword extraction, entity linking and answer type detection, we use cross lingual semantic similarity to extract the answer from knowledge base via relation selection and type matching. We have evaluated our approach on Persian and Spanish which are typologically different languages. Our experiments are on DBPedia. The results are promising for both languages.

1 Introduction

Large scale knowledge bases like DBPedia (Auer et al., 2007) and Freebase (Bollacker et al., 2008) provide structured information in diverse domains. Such resources are worthwhile to answer open-domain questions using structured query. In recent years, answering open-domain questions by querying knowledge bases has gained a lot of attentions (Yahya et al., 2012; Fader et al., 2013; Yih et al., 2014; Dong et al., 2015). These systems exploit many diverse methods like semantic parsing, information extraction (Yao et al., 2014) and deep learning (Yu et al., 2015; Bordes et al., 2015). While existing approaches focused only on English language, there are so many difficulties to cope with in cross lingual setting. On the one hand, lack of tools and resources, and on the other hand, vocabulary gap between source and target languages, frustrate any effort to adapt the existing approaches for languages other than English.

In this paper, we introduce a pipeline of stages for cross lingual question answering over knowledge bases. In the first stage, using a MaxEnt Markov Model, keywords are extracted. Syntactic and semantic features are utilized to do this job. In the second stage, using an SVM classifier, keywords that mention an entity are distinguished from ones that determine the answer type. In the next stage we try to find the most probable entity(s) in KB which can be linked to detected grounded entity(s). Several sources are used to find entities in KB, like abstract of entities in KB, cross lingual dictionaries like BabelNet (Navigli and Ponzetto, 2012) and the KB own cross lingual links (whenever such links exist). Also using extracted keywords we search in the ontology of the KB to predict type of entities that are answers. In the last stage, answers are extracted using two kinds of information: 1. Type of neighbours of found entities 2. Semantic similarity between relation labels of found entities and extracted keywords. Cross lingual semantic similarity are measured using the unified semantic space among languages proposed by Camacho-Collados (2015).

Our system doesn't rely on huge annotated data or any language specific resources except for a chunker. Thus our main contributions are:

Proceedings of the 2016 Workshop on Graph-based Methods for Natural Language Processing, NAACL-HLT 2016, pages 15–19,
San Diego, California, June 17, 2016.

- Introducing a staged cross lingual approach which can easily be adapted to any source language with an available chunker in that language.
- Reducing annotation effort and reliance on huge amount of training data which is a barrier for many resource scarce languages.
- Providing a new QA dataset for Persian and conducting experiences on two different languages.

2 Related Work

Early Question Answering systems like Baseball (Green Jr et al., 1961) were close domain. With the expansion of Linked Open Data, open domain knowledge bases like DBPedia and Freebase emerged. Several approaches have been proposed to provide natural language interface to these KBs. Some of them have utilized semantic parsing techniques (Fader et al., 2014; Cai and Yates, 2013). In these systems the question is converted to an intermediate logical form like lambda calculus and then using this interpretation of the question, the final query is constructed. Some systems have tried to use Information Extraction techniques to overcome QA task (Yao and Durme, 2014; Bordes et al., 2014). Yao and et. al (2014) showed that these two trends are not very different in their performances, but semantic parsing can target answering more compositional questions.

There are some attempts from deep learning researchers in this field (Yu et al., 2015; Yih et al., 2014; Dong et al., 2015). Sukhbaatar and et al. (2015) trained an end-to-end Memory Network contributed by Weston (2014). Their model is multi layered. In each layer any fact has two different input and output embedded form. After passing the embedded question through these layers, the predicted answer is obtained using a weight matrix.

All of aforementioned methods are mono lingual and can not be adapted for a resource scarce language mostly because of their reliance on huge training data or language specific resources both for question understanding or relation and entity extraction. Although cross lingual question answering over unstructured data is a well-known topic (Ahn et al., 2004; de Pablo-Sánchez et al., 2005; Ligozat et al., 2006), but these approaches don't utilize all information available for QA over knowledge bases. Most of these systems deal with multilinguality using fully translation of given question or term-by-term translation of processed question in source language. Entity types and external links to cross lingual resources, existing in well-known open domain KBs, can be exploited to overcome many translation errors and our experiences corroborate this fact. Aggarwal and et al. (2013) proposed a cross lingual QA system over DBPedia. They have achieved 0.481 F_1 on QALD-2. Their system was unable to answer aggregation question. Moreover, unlike our method, they didn't utilize type information in the KB.

3 Method

In this section we introduce our proposed approach to deal with cross lingual QA over KBs. Any given question passes through four stages in a pipeline including 1. Keyword Extraction, 2. Keyword Type Detection, 3. Entity Linking & Ontology Type Extraction, and finally 4. Answer Extraction. We have employed QALD-5 as our dataset for training and testing, and DBPedia 2014 as our KB to extract answers from. We first briefly describe preparing dataset and then explain each of above stages in detail.

3.1 Preparing Dataset

QALD-5 is a multilingual QA dataset over DBPedia 2014 for QALD task at CLEF 2015. It contains 300 training questions in 7 languages with annotated keywords and queries to extract answers from DBPedia and 50 questions as test set. To add Persian translation to these dataset, the questions were translated to Persian by a language expert outside development team. To annotate keywords of each Persian questions we have used majority voting among 5 annotators. Each word has tagged as B, I or O. Also we have augmented this dataset with answer type tag. Each keyword has tagged as type detector or neutral. We have chosen these tags through majority voting among 5 annotators.

3.2 Keyword Extraction

In the first stage, the input question have to be analysed to extract content words which we call them keywords. A MaxEnt Markov Model is used in order to extract these keywords through sequence labelling. The features used to train the model are: 1. Unigram, bigram and trigram of POS tags, 2. Chunk tag, 3. Position of the word in question, 4. IDF of word in corpus [1], 5. Exact match with entity labels in KB and 6. Babelfy tag(Moro et al., 2014).

3.3 Keyword Type Detection

In the second stage each keyword is classified as 1. Type Detector, 2. Grounded Entity or 3. Neutral. To do that we have utilized an SVM classifier with RBF kernel because it has the best performance in 10-fold cross validation in our experiments. The following features are used to train the SVM classifier: 1. Number of words in keyword, 2. POS tags of words in keyword, 3. Position of the first word of the keyword in question, 4. Average IDF of words of keywords in corpus, 5. Exact match with entity labels, 6. Babelfy tag, and 7. Match of translation with ontology types [2].

3.4 Entity Linking & Ontology Type Extraction

When the keywords that must be linked to some entities in the KB or refer to some types in the KB ontology have been found, we should link each of which to its appropriate entity or type. To do entity linking, results of queries over three different collections are merged with different weights and the first result is selected. Queries includes the entity mention augmented by other keywords with different weight and are over: 1. Entity abstracts in language specific chapters of the KB –Only entities which have $sameAs$ links to English version are indexed. For any query, the related English entity is returned. 2. Entity abstracts of English chapter of KB –Any keyword in query is translated to English using Google Translate. and 3. BabelNet –We use Babelfy for entity linking. Weights that cause minimum errors in training samples are chosen for augmenting keywords to queries and merging the results. To link keywords classified as type detector, we use Google Translate to translate the keyword to English and then search in KB ontology. Only string similarity between translated keyword and ontology types is used.

3.5 Answer Extraction

In the last stage using extracted entities, ontology types and keywords classified as Neutral in subsection 3.3, we search in KB graph. All entities in 2-hop vicinity of the found entities in KB whose types are different from extracted ontology types are pruned. If there are entities of desired types with different path labels to the found entities, the cross lingual semantic similarity model contributed by Camacho-Collados (2015) is used to select the most similar relation with the keywords of tagged as Neutral. We have used unified vectores constructed according to BabelNet synsets.

To deal with aggregation questions, we have extracted all questions from the training data with atribute $aggregation = "true"$ and then grouped them in four types:

1. Sort 2. Count 3. Regular expresion 4. Time

For each of these groups, POS tags and words which are common among all members of that group have been extracted and their frequencies have been calculated and normalized. For a given question four scores related to each agregation type is caclulated using following formula:

$$Score_{type}(Q) = \sum_i N(POS_i) * S(POS_i) + \sum_j N(w_j) * S(w_j) \quad (1)$$

$N(*)$ is the number of occurance of $*$ in the question and $S(*)$ is the normalized score obtained for $*$ using agregation training questions. For each type which have some score greater than a threshold, agregation of that type is operated on the final result of the answer extracted. The threshold are calculated using all training questions.

4 Experiments

To evaluate our approach we have conducted experiments on Persian and Spanish. we have used DBPedia 2014 as the KB that answers must be extracted from it. We have tested our system on QALD-5 test set. It contains 49 questions in both languages.

[1] The language specific abstract of every entity in DBPedia was indexed by Lucene to obtain IDF of words.

[2] Keywords are translated to English using Google Translate.

Language(Method)	Precision	Recall	F_1
Persian(ours)	53.3	51.7	52.4
Spanish(ours)	55.2	53.4	54.2
Persian(Fully MT)	30.7	28.3	29.5
Spanish(Fully MT)	33.4	31.1	32.2

Table 1: Performance of our approach for Persian and Spanish questions compared with baseline.

Method	F_1
ours(English)	65.2
Xser(Xu et al., 2014)	63.0

Table 2: Performance of our approach for English questions compared with best participant of QALD-5.

As a baseline we translate each question to English using Google Translate. Table 1 shows the result of our approach for both Persian and Spanish questions compared with results of the baseline. Errors in translating of named entities in fully translating a question is one of main sources of errors in baseline with proportion of 64%.

We have compared the performance of the monolingual version of our approach with the best participant of QALD-5 challenge. Table 2 shows the results. Despite less annotation cost for training the model compared with Xser, our system improved F_1 by 2.2%.

Since our proposed approach consist of a pipeline of pre-processing, we have evaluated internal stages of our system. Table 3 shows the results for each stage. The reported accuracies are average accuracy over 10-fold cross validation.

We have also evaluated the influence of calculating semantic similarity using unified vectors on accuracy of our method. Semantic similarity of the translation of a Persian or Spanish phrase and an English phrase using Word2Vec was used as a baseline. The result for Persian are reported in Table 4.

Stage(Language)	Macro Accuracy
Keyword Extraction(Persian)	92.3
Keyword Extraction(Spanish)	92.8
Keyword Classification(Persian)	88.7
Keyword Classification(Spanish)	89.3
Ontology Type Selection(Persian)	84.4
Ontology Type Selection(Spanish)	85.6
Entity Linking(Persian)	78.6
Entity Linking(Spanish)	79.2
Relation Selection(Persian)	61.8
Relation Selection(Spanish)	63.8

Table 3: Performance of each stage.

Method	F_1
Unified Vectores	52.4
Translation & Word2Vec	46.7

Table 4: Performance of our method with unified vectors and Word2vec semantic similarity

5 Error Analysis

Wrong Relation Selection is the main source of error (32% of errors in test set). Table 3 shows a great accuracy lost between this stage and its previous one. The diversity in paraphrasing different relations in KB is one of most important hindrance to remedy vocabulary gap in this stage even in monolingual setting . Moreover, for some questions the answer are connected to entities grounded in questions by more than one relation. Our approach doesn't select more than one relation.

Other sources of errors include: wrong entity linking (27%), questions with no grounded entity (22%), wrong ontology type selection (15%) and others (4%)

6 Conclusion & Future Works

Question answering over knowledge bases is one of the popular topics for researchers in semantic parsing, information extraction, deep learning and so on. However various systems in recent years have been proposed but cross-linguality is rarely studied so far. In this paper we proposed a cross lingual system using unified semantic representation of concepts in different stages for keyword extraction, keyword classification, entity linking, type extraction and relation selection. Although our experiments show usefulness of proposed approach but there are still a lot of rooms for future works. More investigation on relation extraction is needed. Deep learning approaches like Memory Networks show promising results and we plan to adapt our system for these approaches. Extending our method for other KBs that don't have versions in other languages like Freebase and also other datasets like WebQuestions (Berant et al., 2013) is another room for future work. Recently there was some research on dialect-level differences between Persian and Dari (Malmasi and Dras, 2015). Adapting and evaluating our method in cross-dialect setting has been left for future work.

References

Nitish Aggarwal, Tamara Polajnar, and Paul Buitelaar. 2013. Cross-lingual natural language querying over the web of data. In *NLDB 2013, June 19-21, 2013. Proceedings*, pages 152–163.

Kisuh Ahn, Beatrix Alex, Johan Bos, Tiphaine Dalmas, Jochen L. Leidner, and Matthew Smillie. 2004. Cross-lingual question answering with QED. In *Working Notes for CLEF 2004 Workshop, September 15-17, 2004*.

Sören Auer, Christian Bizer, Georgi Kobilarov, Jens Lehmann, Richard Cyganiak, and Zachary G. Ives. 2007. Dbpedia: A nucleus for a web of open data. In *The Semantic Web,ISWC 2007 + ASWC 2007, November 11-15, 2007.*, pages 722–735.

Jonathan Berant, Andrew Chou, Roy Frostig, and Percy Liang. 2013. Semantic Parsing on Freebase from Question-Answer Pairs. *Proceedings of EMNLP*, pages 1533–1544.

Kurt D. Bollacker, Colin Evans, Praveen Paritosh, Tim Sturge, and Jamie Taylor. 2008. Freebase: a collaboratively created graph database for structuring human knowledge. In *Proceedings of the SIGMOD 2008, June 10-12, 2008*, pages 1247–1250.

Antoine Bordes, Sumit Chopra, and Jason Weston. 2014. Question answering with subgraph embeddings. In *Proceedings of EMNLP 2014, October 25-29, 2014*, pages 615–620.

Antoine Bordes, Nicolas Usunier, Sumit Chopra, and Jason Weston. 2015. Large-scale simple question answering with memory networks. *CoRR*, abs/1506.02075.

Qingqing Cai and Alexander Yates. 2013. Large-scale semantic parsing via schema matching and lexicon extension. In *Proceedings of ACL 2013, 4-9 August 2013, Volume 1: Long Papers*, pages 423–433.

José Camacho-Collados, Mohammad Taher Pilehvar, and Roberto Navigli. 2015. A unified multilingual semantic representation of concepts. In *Proceedings of ACL 2015, July 26-31, 2015, Volume 1: Long Papers*, pages 741–751.

César de Pablo-Sánchez, Ana González-Ledesma, José Luis Martınez-Fernández, José Maria Guirao, Paloma Martinez, and Antonio Moreno. 2005. Miracles 2005 approach to cross-lingual question answering. In *Working Notes of CLEF*.

Li Dong, Furu Wei, Ming Zhou, and Ke Xu. 2015. Question answering over freebase with multi-column convolutional neural networks. In *Proceedings of ACL 2015, July 26-31, 2015, Volume 1: Long Papers*, pages 260–269.

Anthony Fader, Luke S. Zettlemoyer, and Oren Etzioni. 2013. Paraphrase-driven learning for open question answering. In *Proceedings of ACL 2013, 4-9 August 2013, Volume 1: Long Papers*, pages 1608–1618.

Anthony Fader, Luke Zettlemoyer, and Oren Etzioni. 2014. Open question answering over curated and extracted knowledge bases. In *The 20th KDD '14, August 24-27, 2014*, pages 1156–1165.

Bert F Green Jr, Alice K Wolf, Carol Chomsky, and Kenneth Laughery. 1961. Baseball: an automatic question-answerer. In *western joint IRE-AIEE-ACM computer conference*, pages 219–224. ACM.

Anne-Laure Ligozat, Brigitte Grau, Isabelle Robba, and Anne Vilnat. 2006. Evaluation and improvement of cross-lingual question answering strategies. In *Proceedings of the Workshop on Multilingual Question Answering*, pages 23–30. ACL.

Shervin Malmasi and Mark Dras. 2015. Automatic language identification for persian and dari texts. In *Proceedings of PACLING*, pages 59–64.

Andrea Moro, Alessandro Raganato, and Roberto Navigli. 2014. Entity Linking meets Word Sense Disambiguation: a Unified Approach. *TACL*, 2:231–244.

Roberto Navigli and Simone Paolo Ponzetto. 2012. Babelnet: The automatic construction, evaluation and application of a wide-coverage multilingual semantic network. *Artif. Intell.*, 193:217–250.

Sainbayar Sukhbaatar, Jason Weston, Rob Fergus, et al. 2015. End-to-end memory networks. In *NIPS*, pages 2431–2439.

Jason Weston, Sumit Chopra, and Antoine Bordes. 2014. Memory networks. *CoRR*, abs/1410.3916.

Kun Xu, Yansong Feng, and Dongyan Zhao. 2014. Answering natural language questions via phrasal semantic parsing. In *Working Notes for CLEF 2014 Conference, September 15-18, 2014.*, pages 1260–1274.

Mohamed Yahya, Klaus Berberich, Shady Elbassuoni, Maya Ramanath, Volker Tresp, and Gerhard Weikum. 2012. Natural language questions for the web of data. In *Proceedings of EMNLP-CoNLL July 12-14, 2012*, pages 379–390.

Xuchen Yao and Benjamin Van Durme. 2014. Information extraction over structured data: Question answering with freebase. In *Proceedings of ACL 2014, June 22-27, 2014, Volume 1: Long Papers*, pages 956–966.

Xuchen Yao, Jonathan Berant, and Benjamin Van Durme. 2014. Freebase QA: Information Extraction or Semantic Parsing? *Proceedings of the ACL 2014 Workshop on Semantic Parsing*, pages 82–86.

Wen-tau Yih, Xiaodong He, and Christopher Meek. 2014. Semantic parsing for single-relation question answering. In *Proceedings of ACL 2014, June 22-27, 2014, Volume 2: Short Papers*, pages 643–648.

Yang Yu, Wei Zhang, Chung-Wei Hang, and Bowen Zhou. 2015. Empirical study on deep learning models for question answering. *CoRR*, abs/1510.07526.

Network Motifs May Improve Quality Assessment of Text Documents

Thomas Arnold and **Karsten Weihe**
Research Training Group AIPHES / Algorithmic Group
Department of Computer Science, Technische Universität Darmstadt
Hochschulstrasse 10, 64289 Darmstadt, Germany
arnold@aiphes.tu-darmstadt.de, weihe@cs.tu-darmstadt.de

Abstract

Motif analysis counts the number of small building blocks (the *motifs*) in a network and relates these statistical numbers to the inherent semantics of the network. In the realm of natural language processing, the networks are induced by texts. We demonstrate that motif analysis may help assess the quality of a document. More specifically, we consider the German Wikipedia and use the label "featured" as the (binary) quality criterion. The length (number of words) of an article is a comparatively good predictor for this label. We show that a well-designed combination of this criterion and motif statistics yields a significant improvement. We also found that a deeper look into the most relevant motifs may improve our understanding of quality.

1 Introduction

Recent work has shown that *motif analysis* is quite promising for natural language processing (Biemann et al., 2012; Mesgar and Strube, 2015). Roughly speaking, the occurrences of small subgraphs like those in Figure 1 are counted, and relations between this *motif signature* and the semantics of the network are analyzed. We adapt this technique to the assessment of document quality. Our computational study is based on the German Wikipedia. The label "featured" indicates high quality. A certain combination with the length of an article, which is a very good predictor for an article's quality in this specific sense (Blumenstock, 2008), yields a significant improvement over the length alone.

This paper is organized as follows. First we briefly sketch our contribution in Section 1.1. Then, in Section 2, we discuss the state of the art and explain the concept of motif analysis. We illustrate the composition of our corpus in Section 3 and details of our approach in Section 4. Quantitative and qualitative results are presented in Section 5 and 6, respectively. Finally, we summarize our work and outline next steps in Section 7.

1.1 Our Contribution

The research questions In this paper, we address three general questions:

1. *Quantitative*: does motif analysis as a stand-alone tool help us assess the quality of text documents statistically?
2. *Quantitative*: does it help us in conjunction with other quality measures?
3. *Qualitative*: does it help us understand the nature of quality any better?

The German Wikipedia is our basis. The Wikipedia allows the community to assign the label "featured" to an article via an extensive communication and revision process, based on a collection of stylistic and content-based quality criteria. We use the distinction featured / non-featured as a (binary) quality criterion. Our corpus comprises all featured articles and a purely random selection of non-featured articles such that 7% of all articles in our corpus are featured.

In summary, we address the three general research questions in the following specific form: does motif

Proceedings of the 2016 Workshop on Graph-based Methods for Natural Language Processing, NAACL-HLT 2016, pages 20–28,
San Diego, California, June 17, 2016. ©2016 Association for Computational Linguistics

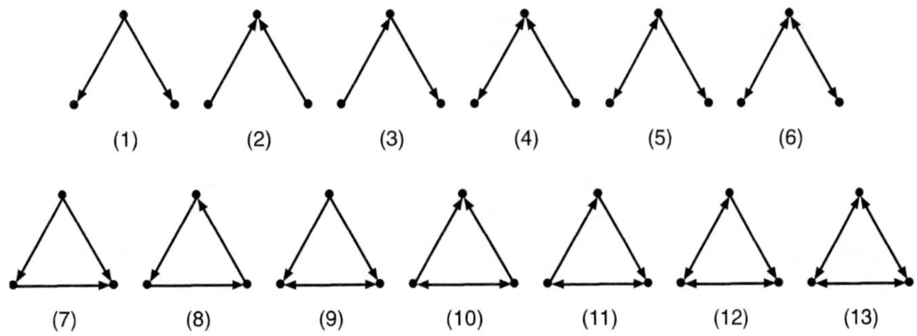

Figure 1: the directed motifs on three nodes. A double arrow indicates the presence of two mutually opposite arcs.

analysis help us – alone or in conjunction with another criterion – to distinguish between featured and non-featured articles, and if so, does it yield a deeper understanding of the nature of featured articles?

The bare length of an article is a surprisingly good predictor for whether or not an article is featured. So, for the second research question, we will combine the article length with our motif analysis.

Methodological contribution The revision history of a Wikipedia article allows us to analyze the development of the induced network and its motif signature over time. So, for each article we analyzed a series of "snapshots" and the temporal tendency of the motif signature.

2 Related Work and Background

2.1 Related Work

Network analysis of text documents There is a large scientific body of methods and applications of network analysis (Aggarwal and Wang, 2010; Aggarwal, 2011). Graph mining – the art of detecting and analyzing patterns and structures in graphs – is the specific focus of the surveys (Cook and Holder, 2006; Fortunato, 2010).

It seems reasonable to classify network analysis techniques by the level of granularity they address. Elementary statistical measures such as the node degree distribution operate on the level of single nodes and edges. In the opposite extreme case, on the global level, the structure of a network is captured in a single (scalar) numerical value. Examples for global measures are the average shortest path length, the diameter, as well as simple characteristics such as node and edge count. See the above-mentioned surveys for a systematic discussion.

Motif analysis Motifs such as those in Figure 1 capture local structure and are thus, in a sense, on an intermediate level between measures on single nodes and edges on one hand and global measures on the other hand.

Motif analysis has first been investigated in computational biology (Shen-Orr et al., 2002) and has since been applied to a variety of network types in biology and biochemistry (Schreiber and Schwöbbermeyer, 2010). The underlying insight is that biological and biochemical dynamics are statistically related to the occurrence of small functional blocks, which have specific structures. This insight is well captured by motif signatures, and in fact, many computational studies reveal significant relations. Due to this success, it did not take long time until this technique has been applied to networks from other domains. For example, (Milo et al., 2002; Milo et al., 2004) compare networks from biology, electrical engineering, natural language and computer science and find that the motif signatures from different domains are so different that they may serve as a "fingerprint" of the respective domain. Krumov et al. (2011) use motif analysis on coauthorship networks to find relations between particular motifs and citation frequency. They reveal one particular motif that implies high average citation frequency, and provide explanations based on social processes that are covered by the network.

Tran et al. (2015) explored differences in directed and undirected networks of various disciplines, including ecology, biology and social science. They conclude that motifs in undirected networks are very similar. However, motif analysis of directed networks was able to distinguish networks from different fields. Furthermore, larger motifs captured more information about individual differences than small motifs.

Quite recently, motif analysis has been applied to text processing. In (Biemann et al., 2012), human-written texts and artificial texts with quite similar characteristics were compared by means of the motif signatures of certain induced networks. For several natural languages, the motif signatures were so different that they alone were sufficient to distinguish the human-written from the artificial texts.

Mesgar and Strube (2015) applied motif analysis to Wall Street Journal news articles. These texts were represented as a combined entity and discourse relation graph. They identified several motifs that are highly correlated with manual readability ratings.

Quality of documents Defining and measuring the quality of a document in a formalized way is an intrinsically difficult task. Various mathematical measures have been proposed for individual aspects of quality, like correct grammar (Tetreault and Chodorow, 2008) or spelling (Brill and Moore, 2000). Another part of quality, information ordering, has been evaluated with rank correlation metrics (Lapata, 2006). Louis and Nenkova (2013) investigated text quality at a much broader level that incorporates features of emotions and surprise.

A network based approach on quality assessment of school essays was presented by (Antiqueira et al., 2007). This research used global statistical network features of text-induced graphs, including mean clustering coefficient and average shortest path length. The authors presented correlations between these metrics and manually annotated quality scores.

2.2 Background: Networks and Motifs

Graphs vs. networks All graphs in this paper are directed. Basically, we use the terms *graph* and *network* synonymously. However, we will speak of *networks* only if the nodes and edges have a meaning in the application context.

More specifically, in our work, the nodes of a network are the sentences of a document, and two nodes are connected by an edge if, and only if, the two represented sentences have at least one noun in common and are separated by at most two other sentences. The direction of the edge reflects the relative order of the sentences in the document, from the earlier to the later sentence. Such a definition of directed edges, which combines content with locality, has turned out to be quite promising.

Motif analysis A *motif* is simply a small connected graph – typically, but not exclusively, with three or four nodes. Figure 1 shows all directed motifs on three nodes.[1]

For a *motif analysis* of a set of networks, a set of pairwise non-isomorphic motifs is to be firmly selected a priori. To analyze a network N, the number of occurrences of each motif in N is counted. In that, an *occurrence* of a motif M in N is a set X of nodes of N such that the subgraph of N induced by X is isomorphic to M.[2] Since no two motifs are isomorphic, each set of nodes of N can be the occurrence of at most one motif. And in fact, even if a motif bears some symmetries such as (1), (2), (6), (8), (9), (10), and (13) in Figure 1, the underlying node set is counted as *one* occurrence only.

The *motif signature* of a network N with respect to a selection of motifs comprises the number of occurrences of every selected motif in N, scaled to a sum of 1.

Generally speaking, *motif analysis* relates the structure of a network to the investigated semantic properties of the network, which are induced by the application context. There is a quantitative and a qualitative side to this. The *quantitative* analysis identifies statistical relations between the motif signature and the semantic properties. On the other hand, the *qualitative* analysis is based on the idea that the motifs – if well selected – may be interpreted as building blocks of the network, and that an unexpectedly high or low frequency of some motifs may yield a deeper understanding of these semantic properties.

[1]Unfortunately, the terminology is not consistent throughout the scientific literature: in many articles, only the selected subgraphs with unexpectedly high frequency in a network are called *motifs* of the networks', and the subgraphs with unexpectedly low frequency are then called *anti-motifs*.

[2]Let $G_1 = (V_1, E_1)$ and $G_2 = (V_2, E_2)$ be two directed graphs such that $|V_1| \leq |V_2|$, and let $V_2' \subseteq V_2$ such that $|V_2'| = |V_1|$. Then G_1 is the *subgraph* of G_2 *induced by* V_2' if there is a bijection $\varphi : V_1 \to V_2'$ such that for all $x, y \in V_1$, it is $(x, y) \in E_1$ if and only if $(\varphi(x), \varphi(y)) \in E_2$.

3 Data

Our corpus is a subset of the German Wikipedia. We utilize the quality label "featured" as an indicator for high quality articles. Therefore, we include all $2,338$ featured articles of a complete snapshot of the German Wikipedia from June 2015. The proportion of featured articles in this snapshot is 0.13%. Adding all non-featured articles would result in a dataset of very large proportions and with an extremely skewed distribution of the relevant "featured" label. This is a huge problem for most machine learning techniques. We deal with this problem by under-sampling the overrepresented class (Drummond et al., 2003). For this reason, we restricted the set of all non-featured articles to a purely random – and thus representative – sample of $33,295$ articles, which increases the share of featured articles in our corpus to 7.02%.

For each article in our corpus, we selected 10 distinct article versions from the article's revision history. A new version of an article is created every time submitted revisions or additions to this article are approved by the community. For every featured article, we split all of its article versions into a set of versions with the featured label and a set of version without the featured label. On average, this divides the versions of a featured article into about 57% non-featured versions and 43% featured versions. For every featured article, we select five random versions from each part.

We split the versions of non-featured articles similarly into "early" and "late" parts of the revision history with the same proportions as the featured articles' featured and non-featured parts. This way, we pick five random versions from the earliest 57% versions of a non-featured article, and five random versions from the latest 43% versions.

For every article version, we create a network according to our graph representation, search the network for motifs and compute the corresponding motif signatures, as explained below.

4 Our Approach

Graph representation We use a sentence level graph representation based on shared nouns.

For every selected version of a selected Wikipedia article, we construct a network $G = (V, E)$ with

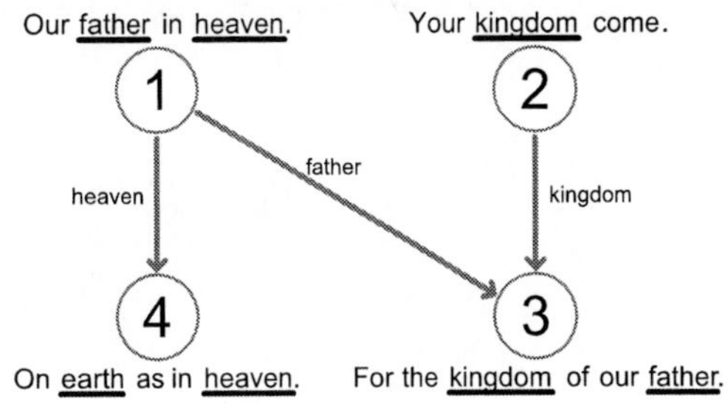

Figure 2: Exemplary graph representation with four consecutive sentences.

a set of nodes V and a set of directed edges E as follows:

The nodes of this network are the sentences of the article version. Two nodes are connected by an edge if and only if these two conditions are fulfilled:

1. There exists at least one noun token that appears in both corresponding sentences.

2. The two sentences are separated by at most two other sentences in the document.

Edges are directed and point from the sentence earlier in the text to the latter one. Figure 2 shows an example of this representation.

Motif analysis To each network created from a Wikipedia article version, we apply a motif analysis. In our case, we search for subgraphs of three or four connected nodes. Furthermore, we only search for motifs of three or four directly consecutive sentences. With this constraint, we can only discover discourse connections of sentences that follow right after each other. Because of their close proximity, we can be pretty sure that these sentences have a strong discourse connection and are likely to share a common topic to some extent.

The resulting motifs are quite rare. If we relaxed this constraint and searched for all connected subgraphs of three or four nodes, the number of occurrences of motifs increases significantly. However, we found that the motif analysis yields worse results.

The way our networks are constructed limits the number of possible subgraphs considerably. The directions of the edges have to follow the order of appearance of the corresponding sentences, which

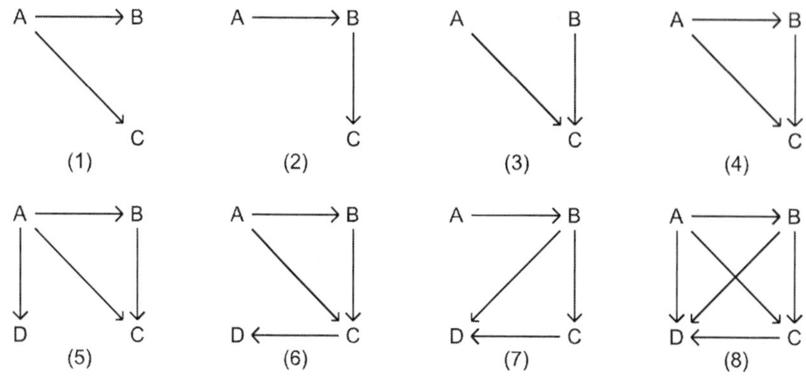

Figure 3: All possible directed motifs on three nodes, and four selected motifs on four nodes.

rules out every form of loops. All four possible connected subgraphs on three nodes and four subgraphs (out of 42) on four nodes are shown in Figure3.

The node order together with the adjacency condition allows for very efficient searching for these motifs with a sliding window. The occurrences of all three-node motifs and all four-node motifs are scaled to a sum of 1, respectively. The results build the motif signatures, as defined in Section 2.2.

Machine learning setup We use the values of the motif signatures as 46 numeric features for our machine learning experiments. In addition, we include the word count of the article version as an additional baseline feature according to (Blumenstock, 2008), for comparison and combination. The experiments were performed with J48, a Java implementation of the C4.5 tree learning algorithm, included in Weka (Witten et al., 1999; Quinlan, 2014). The tree structures allow us to interpret the model and analyze the most determining features. We use default parameters with the exception of "minNumObj", the minimum number of instances per leaf. The default value of this parameter is 2. We set it to 100 to reduce overfitting effect, and will present results for both configurations. The evaluation is performed with 10-fold cross validation over 10 experiment iterations.

5 Quantitative Results

Baseline Our corpus contains 7% featured article versions. Therefore, consistently predicting the majority class "non-featured" produces a lower bound baseline accuracy of 0.93. The baseline we want to compare with is created by a J48 experiment with the word count feature only, which achieves 0.95 accuracy.

Stand-alone We evaluate the predictive power of our motifs with experiments that use only 3-node motifs, only 4-node motifs or both. The results for these experiments with default number of 2 instances per leaf are presented in Table 1. Experiments with all 3-node motifs without word count could not reach the baseline, but using all 4-node motifs without word count performed much better at 0.9745 accuracy. This includes significant overfitting effects, as the corresponding tree model is very large and consists of over 3,000 nodes and leafs.

Used Features	Accuracy	Tree size
Majority class baseline	0.93	
3N + 4N	0.9748	3605
4N	0.9745	3598
W (baseline)	0.95	6
3N	0.9488	1417

Table 1: J48 results for motifs alone, parameter minNumObj = 2, W = word count, 3N = all 3-node motifs, 4N = all 4-node motifs

Table 2 shows the results with 100 minimum instances per leaf (up from 2), which reduces the model size and the overfitting effects. Lower bound and baseline accuracy are the same as in the first setup, at 0.93 and 0.95, respectively. In this setup, using only 3-node motifs yields an accuracy of 0.943. 4-node motifs alone or in conjunction with 3-node motifs do not outperform the word count base-

Used Features	Accuracy	Tree size
Majority class baseline	0.93	
3N + 4N	0.9508	217
4N	0.9504	188
W (baseline)	0.95	3
3N	0.943	140

Table 2: J48 results for motifs alone, parameter minNumObj = 100, W = word count, 3N = all 3-node motifs, 4N = all 4-node motifs

Used Features	Accuracy	Tree size
Majority class baseline	0.93	
W + 3N + 4N	0.96	179
W + 4N	0.9577	200
W + 3N	0.9542	59
W (baseline)	0.95	3

Table 4: J48 results for combination, parameter minNumObj = 100, W = word count, 3N = all 3-node motifs, 4N = all 4-node motifs

line considerably, either. We conclude that our motif analysis as a stand-alone tool did not lead to notable statistical improvements.

Combination In our experiments, we also combined the baseline feature word count with motif features. The results for these combinations are shown in Table 3 with default number of 2 instances per leaf and Table 4 with 100 instances per leaf. At default setup, a combination of word count with 3-node and 4-node motifs shows excellent performance at 0.978 accuracy. Again, very large decision tree models were created, which indicates overfitting. Limiting the tree size reduces the decision tree to very moderate size and still results in 0.96 accuracy. Motifs together with word count close the gap from the baseline's 5% miscategorized examples to 4%.

Used Features	Accuracy	Tree size
Majority class baseline	0.93	
W + 3N + 4N	0.9780	3179
W + 4N	0.9779	3254
W + 3N	0.9567	847
W (baseline)	0.95	6

Table 3: J48 results for combination, parameter minNumObj = 2, W = word count, 3N = all 3-node motifs, 4N = all 4-node motifs

We confirmed this improvement and its statistical significance on reduced subsets of our data, and also in a balanced setting. We created the reduced subsets by a purely random selection of 10% featured and non-featured article versions. Compared to the full dataset, these subsets have reduced size, but the same ratio of featured vs. non-featured instances. To create balanced subsets, we combined all featured article versions and an equal amount of randomly selected, non-featured article versions. We constructed 20 subsets for both settings to measure variance and calculate statistical significance. See Table 5 for the results of the reduced subsets, and Table 6 for the results of the balanced scenario.

Used Features	Mean acc.	Standard dev.
W + 3N + 4N	95.116	0.073
W + 4N	95.093	0.071
W + 3N	95.079	0.085
W (baseline)	94.741	0.096

Table 5: Mean accuracy and standard deviation for 20 reduced datasets, J48 parameter minNumObj = 100, W = word count, 3N = all 3-node motifs, 4N = all 4-node motifs

Used Features	Mean acc.	Standard dev.
W + 3N + 4N	94.963	0.111
W + 4N	94.941	0.124
W + 3N	94.852	0.107
W (baseline)	94.44	0.109

Table 6: Mean accuracy and standard deviation for 20 balanced datasets, J48 parameter minNumObj = 100, W = word count, 3N = all 3-node motifs, 4N = all 4-node motifs

Due to the reduced amount of data, the mean accuracy was lower compared to previous experiments with same features and parameters, but the order remained constant. The accuracy is very stable with respect to data composition, with standard deviations between only 0.073 and 0.124. The mean accuracy of every combination setup surpassed the baseline by at least three standard deviations. Computation of p-values confirmed that all results are statistically highly significant at $p < 0.001$.

Motif	Accuracy
(4)	95.1713845
(8)	95.1328903
(3)	95.0983271
(1)	95.080967
(7)	94.9560177
(2)	94.9386417

Table 7: Accuracy of J48 experiments with single motifs in combination with word count

Most dominant motifs The motifs with highest impact on quality are obtained with two different methods.

To determine the most effective motifs in our machine learning setup, we performed additional experiments with single motifs in combination with word count. Table 7 displays the results with highest accuracy, which indicates a connection between these motifs and quality. The motif labels correspond to Figure 3.

As a second approach, we directly evaluated the correlation of the motif signatures to the quality label of the corresponding text. Since our variable for quality is dichotomous, we use the point biserial correlation coefficient. The value distribution of our motif signature entries imposes potential problems for this computation. An example of this distribution is shown in Figure 4. We see large proportions of the extreme values 0 and 1 in our motif signature distributions. A value of 1 in the signature can only happen if the respective motif was the only motif to be found, which only happens in very small texts. A 0 entry also hints to small texts, as large texts tend to contain at least a fraction of every motif type. Small articles in Wikipedia are rarely featured, so both extreme values of the distribution largely correspond to non-featured articles, which distorts the point biserial correlation coefficient. To eliminate the effects of article length in the correlations, we create subcollections of featured and non-featured article versions with similar amounts of motifs, measured by mean average values and standard deviation.

We found two motifs with a distinctively negative correlation to the featured quality label, and three motifs with distinctively positive correlation coefficients. See Table 8 for these results. All these motifs have also been identified by our machine learning approach, which confirms our findings. We concentrated our qualitative interpretation on the motifs with most dominant results, which are motifs (1), (3), (4) and (8) of Fig 3.

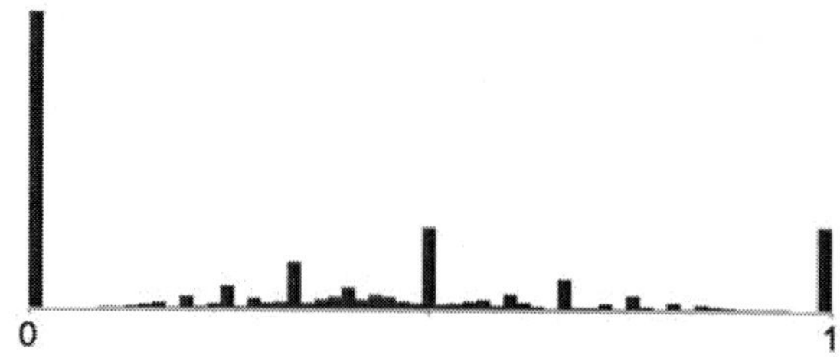

Figure 4: Distribution of values for motif (4) over all motif signatures.

Motif	Correlation
(1)	0.2015307459
(3)	0.1847741318
(2)	0.1803760107
(8)	-0.2691052665
(4)	-0.27433768

Table 8: All motifs with correlation coefficient of absolute value > 0.15

6 Qualitative Results

The two motifs that are most positively correlated with the featured quality label are motifs (1) and (3). The huge amount of data made an exhaustive investigation of all motif occurrences infeasible. Therefore, we examined random examples of these motifs in our data set.

Many examples of motif (1) showed this sentence structure: The first sentence introduces two connected entities; the second sentence offers details about the first entity; the third sentence explains the other entity. One example from the German Wikipedia:

(a) Von den drei Hartstrahlen der Rückenflosse wurde der erste zur Angel (Illicium) mit anhängendem Köder (Esca) umgebildet.

(b) Das Illicium hat oft eine Streifenzeichnung.

(c) Die Esca hat bei den einzelnen Anglerfischarten eine unterschiedliche Form und ist ein wichtiges Unterscheidungsmerkmal zwischen den Arten.

Analyzing motif (3) revealed a similar, but decisively different pattern: The first sentence introduces one entity, the second sentence introduces a second one. The last sentence combines the two mentions and draws a connection.

(a) Die Haupthenne bleibt mit dem Hahn oft über mehrere Jahre zusammen.

(b) Bei den Nebenhennen handelt es sich meistens um recht junge Weibchen.

(c) Der Hahn paart sich zunächst mit der Haupthenne, sodann mit den Nebenhennen.

These two ways to introduce and connect entities are an indication of good writing style. The reader can see explanations for the two mentioned entities and their connection in direct vicinity. This makes it easy to understand and to follow the argument structure.

Motifs (4) and (8) are highly negatively correlated with the Wikipedia article quality. They share a very similar structure: Motif (4) is a maximally connected 3-node subgraph, motif (8) is a maximally connected 4-node subgraph. Many text examples of these motifs share a pattern of repetition. One noun is used three or four times in a row in very close proximity.

(a) Die Nahrungssuche erfolgt in der Regel einzeln, seltener als Paar.

(b) Bei Beobachtungen waren die Tiere in 92 % aller Fälle allein auf Nahrungssuche.

(c) Beutejagd und Nahrungssuche bestehen vor allem darin, dass die Füchse ihre Beute zumeist zwischen und unter Steinen suchen und gelegentlich auch graben.

Repetition is a strong stylistic device that can enhance learning effects, but it can also make the text tedious and reduce the attention of a reader (Grill-Spector et al., 2006; Tannen, 2007). Too much repetition is a sign of bad writing style and is certainly avoided in good articles, as our findings demonstrate.

7 Conclusion and Outlook

We have seen that motif analysis can improve the assessment – and our understanding – of the quality of a document. For that, we explored one particular setting and presented the results in this paper. We formulated the following research questions:

1. *Quantitative*: does motif analysis as a stand-alone tool help us assess the quality of text documents statistically?

2. *Quantitative*: does it help us in conjunction with other quality measures?

3. *Qualitative*: does it help us understand the nature of quality any better?

Our empirical findings In our corpus, only 7% of all articles are featured. Hence, categorizing *all* articles as non-featured gives quite a high base line. If the threshold is well chosen, the word count of an article miscategorizes 5%.

Our motif analysis alone is not better than that, so the answer to the first research question is not strictly positive. However, we showed that our combination of both criteria reduces the share of miscategorized articles from 5% down to 4%.

For our third research question, we identified a subset of motifs with high positive or negative correlation to the featured label. Two motifs occur outstandingly frequently in the featured articles, and two other motifs occur outstandingly frequently in the non-featured articles. All four motifs are indeed indicators of text quality as desired: the two former ones are frequently induced by two concepts of good writing style, whereas the two latter ones are frequently induced by two cases of repetitive style.

Future work In the future, we will extend our work to other concepts of quality. However, we anticipate that other quality criteria will require completely different approaches with different networks and, possibly, even different sets of motifs.

Acknowledgments

This work has been supported by the German Research Foundation as part of the Research Training Group Adaptive Preparation of Information from

Heterogeneous Sources (AIPHES) under grant No. GRK 1994/1."

References

Charu C. Aggarwal and Haixun Wang. 2010. Managing and mining graph data. *Database*, 40:487–513.

Charu C Aggarwal. 2011. *Social Network Data Analytics*. Kluwer.

Lucas Antiqueira, M das Gracas V Nunes, ON Oliveira Jr, and L da F Costa. 2007. Strong correlations between text quality and complex networks features. *Physica A: Statistical Mechanics and its Applications*, 373:811–820.

Chris Biemann, Stefanie Roos, and Karsten Weihe. 2012. Quantifying semantics using complex network analysis. In *COLING 2012*.

Joshua E Blumenstock. 2008. Size matters: word count as a measure of quality on wikipedia. In *Proceedings of the 17th international conference on World Wide Web*, pages 1095–1096. ACM.

Eric Brill and Robert C Moore. 2000. An improved error model for noisy channel spelling correction. In *Proceedings of the 38th Annual Meeting on Association for Computational Linguistics*, pages 286–293. Association for Computational Linguistics.

D. J. Cook and L. B. Holder. 2006. *MIning Graph Data*. Wiley.

Chris Drummond, Robert C Holte, et al. 2003. C4. 5, class imbalance, and cost sensitivity: why undersampling beats over-sampling. In *Workshop on learning from imbalanced datasets II*, volume 11.

Santo Fortunato. 2010. Community detection in graphs. *Physics Reports*, 486:75–174.

Kalanit Grill-Spector, Richard Henson, and Alex Martin. 2006. Repetition and the brain: neural models of stimulus-specific effects. *Trends in cognitive sciences*, 10(1):14–23.

Lachezar Krumov, Christoph Fretter, Matthias Müller-Hannemann, Karsten Weihe, and Marc-Thorsten Hütt. 2011. Motifs in co-authorship networks and their relation to the impact of scientific publications. *European Physical Journal B*, 84(4):535–540.

Mirella Lapata. 2006. Automatic evaluation of information ordering: Kendall's tau. *Computational Linguistics*, 32(4):471–484.

Annie Louis and Ani Nenkova. 2013. What makes writing great? first experiments on article quality prediction in the science journalism domain. *Transactions of the Association for Computational Linguistics*, 1:341–352.

Mohsen Mesgar and Michael Strube. 2015. Graph-based coherence modeling for assessing readability. *Lexical and Computational Semantics (* SEM 2015)*, page 309.

R. Milo, S. Shen-Orr, S. Itzkovitz, N. Kashtan, D. Chklovskii, and U. Alon. 2002. Network Motifs: Simple Building Blocks of Complex Networks. *Science*, 298(5594):824–827, October.

R. Milo, S. Itzkovitz, N. Kashtan, R. Levitt, S. Shen-Orr, I. Ayzenshtat, M. Sheffer, and U. Alon. 2004. Superfamilies of evolved and designed networks. *Science*, 303(5663):1538–1542, March.

J Ross Quinlan. 2014. *C4. 5: programs for machine learning*. Elsevier.

Falk Schreiber and Henning Schwöbbermeyer. 2010. *Statistical and Evolutionary Analysis of Biological Network Data*, chapter Motifs in biological networks, pages 45–64. Imperial College Press/World Scientific.

S.S. Shen-Orr, R. Milo, S. Mangan, and U. Alon. 2002. Network motifs in the transcriptional regulation network of Escherichia coli. *Nature genetics*, 31(1):64–68.

Deborah Tannen. 2007. *Talking voices: Repetition, dialogue, and imagery in conversational discourse*, volume 26. Cambridge University Press.

Joel R. Tetreault and Martin Chodorow. 2008. The ups and downs of preposition error detection in esl writing. In *Proceedings of the 22Nd International Conference on Computational Linguistics - Volume 1*, COLING '08, pages 865–872, Stroudsburg, PA, USA. Association for Computational Linguistics.

Ngoc Tam L Tran, Luke DeLuccia, Aidan F McDonald, and Chun-Hsi Huang. 2015. Cross-disciplinary detection and analysis of network motifs. *Bioinformatics and Biology insights*, 9:49.

Ian H Witten, Eibe Frank, Len Trigg, Mark Hall, Geoffrey Holmes, and Sally Jo Cunningham. 1999. Weka: Practical machine learning tools and techniques with java implementations.

Better Together: Combining Language and Social Interactions into a Shared Representation

Yi-Yu Lai* **Chang Li*** **Dan Goldwasser** **Jennifer Neville**
Department of Computer Science,
Purdue University, West Lafayette, Indiana
{lai49, li1873, dgoldwas, neville}@purdue.edu
* authors contributed equally

Abstract

Despite the clear inter-dependency between analyzing the interactions in social networks, and analyzing the natural language content of these interactions, these aspects are typically studied independently. In this paper we present a first step towards finding a joint representation, by embedding the two aspects into a single vector space. We show that the new representation can help improve performance in two social relations prediction tasks.

1 Introduction

The interactions, social bonds and relationships between people have been studied extensively in recent years. Broadly speaking, these works fall into two, almost completely disconnected, camps. The first, focusing on *social network analysis*, looks at the network structure and information flow on it as means of inferring knowledge about the network. For example, works by (Leskovec et al., 2008; Kumar et al., 2010) model the evolution of network structure over time, and works such as (Xiang et al., 2010; Leskovec et al., 2010) use the network structure to predict properties of links (e.g., strength, sign).

The second camp, focusing on *natural language analysis*, looks into tasks such as extracting social relationships from narrative text (Elson et al., 2010; Van De Camp and van den Bosch, 2011; Agarwal et al., 2012) and analyzing the contents of the information flowing through the network. For example, works by (Danescu-Niculescu-Mizil et al., 2012; Hassan et al., 2012; Filippova, 2012; Volkova et al., 2014; West et al., 2014; Rahimi et al., 2015; Volkova et al., 2015) extract attributes of, and social relationships between, nodes by analyzing the textual communication between them. Other works (Krishnan and Eisenstein, 2014; Sap et al., 2014) use the social network to inform language analysis.

Both perspectives on social network analysis resulted in a wide range of successful applications; however, they neglect to model the interactions between the social and linguistic representations and how they complement one another. One of the few exceptions was discussed in (West et al., 2014), which inferred sentiment links between nodes in a social network by jointly modeling the local output probabilities of a sentiment analyzer looking at the textual interactions between the nodes and the global network structure. While resulting in better performance, inference is done over two *independent* representations, one capturing the linguistic information, and the other, the network structure.

Instead, in this paper we take the first step towards finding a joint representation over both linguistic and network information, rather than treating the two independently. We follow the intuition that interactions in a social network can be fully captured only by taking into account both types of information together. To achieve this goal, we embed the input social graph into a dense, continuous, low-dimensional vector space, capturing both network and linguistic similarities between nodes. Word (Mikolov et al., 2013; Pennington et al., 2014) and Network (Perozzi et al., 2014; Tang et al., 2015) embedding approaches that were recently proposed, aim to combat a similar problem in their respective domains–data sparsity. Both follow a similar approach–embed discrete objects (words or nodes in

Proceedings of the 2016 Workshop on Graph-based Methods for Natural Language Processing, NAACL-HLT 2016, pages 29–33,
San Diego, California, June 17, 2016.

the graph) into a continuous vector representation, based on the context they appear in. Our approach aims to map both social and linguistic information into the same vector space, rather than embedding the two aspects into two independent spaces. The social graph, originally containing only quantitative properties of the interaction between nodes (e.g., number of messages exchanged between nodes), is extended to capture the contents of these interactions, by computing the textual similarity between the messages generated by each one of the nodes. The computed similarity is used to weight the edges between adjacent nodes. We embed the modified graph nodes into a vector space, using the embedding technique described by (Tang et al., 2015).

We evaluate the joint representation by using it in two social relationship prediction tasks and comparing it to several different word-based and network based representations. Our experiments show the advantage of the joint representation.

2 Problem Formulation

Our primary assumption is there is a latent space that influences the interactions we observe among people. Thus the goal of our work is to learn this latent representation from the observed data. We describe the data and problem more specifically below.

2.1 Data

We assume that the data comprise a graph $G = (V, E)$, where nodes V correspond to entities (e.g., users in a social network), and the edges E correspond to textual interactions among the entities (e.g., emails, messages). Each edge $e^t_{ij} \in E$, which refers to a message sent from node v_i to node v_j at time t, has an associated document representation d^t_{ij}. We refer to the set of messages (documents) between nodes v_i and v_j as $\mathbf{E}_{ij} := \{e^t_{ij}\}_t$ ($\mathbf{D}_{ij}$ respectively). Moreover, we refer to the set of messages (documents) sent by a node v_i to any other node as $\mathbf{E}_i := \{e^t_{ij}\}_{t,j}$ ($\mathbf{D}_i$ respectively).

2.2 Motivation

Given this type of network data, the goal is to discover the underlying latent representation of the nodes. Our assumption is that the entities are embedded in a latent space that influences the frequency and nature of their communication. We assume that each node has a location in space (e.g., in $\mathbf{R}^2$, the location of v_i is $\mathbf{v}_i := (x_i, y_i)$), and that pairwise node distances (e.g., $d(\mathbf{v}_i, \mathbf{v}_j)$) affect the likelihood of communication and the content of that communication. More specifically, we assume that nearby nodes are more likely to communicate, and talk about similar things. Thus, we assume the latent space embedding represents entities' interests and pairs of entities with similar interests are more likely to interact. These assumptions are motivated by online communities where users exhibit *homophily* (McPherson et al., 2001), i.e., users with common interests are more likely to form relationships.

2.3 Problem Definition

Given the framework and assumptions described above, we can now state the problem definition for the work in this paper. Assume as input, a multi-graph $G = (V, E)$ with messages between nodes in the graph that can be modeled as a set of documents. The goal is to learn an embedding of the nodes V in $\mathbf{R}^\mathbf{k}$ such that the representation reflects both the frequency and content of the messages.

To achieve this we will consider several different ways to compute the embedding based on optimizing (1) network connectivity, (2) message content, and (3) connectivity and content. Our conjecture is that jointly considering connectivity and content will produce an embedding that is more robust to noisy interaction data. Strong (but introverted) friends may talk less frequently but share more common interests, compared to gregarious users who talk more frequently but with many (weak) friends.

Since there is no ground truth for quantitative evaluation, it is difficult to directly evaluate the quality of a learned embedding. Thus, we evaluate our methods indirectly via related classification tasks. In this work, we will use the learned embeddings in two link-based prediction tasks, where we differentiate (1) strong vs. weak(er) friendships, and (2) employees working in the same vs. different groups.

3 Method

The input for our task is the text-enriched network graph G. The goal is to compute a node embedding from G and then use the embedding to generate features for pairs of nodes, which can then be used for a prediction task. The process follows these steps.

• **Textual-Similarity (TS) Infused Social Graph:** Construct graph weights $\mathbf{W}_{ij}$ based on the text in G, according to **(1)** a *Node* or *Edge* view of the documents, and **(2)** using *Topic Model* or *Word Embedding* to represent the content.

• **Node Embedding:** Construct an embedding function $V \rightarrow R^k$, mapping the (weighted) graph nodes into a R^k dimensional space. We used the LINE method (Tang et al., 2015). We omit the details due to space restrictions.

• **Feature Extraction:** Construct a feature set for each node pair, using 9 similarity measures between the nodes' k-dimensional vector representations from the embedding. We experiment with additional features extracted directly.

3.1 Creating the TS-Infused Social Graph

The TS-Infused social graph captures the interaction between node pairs by modifying the strength of the edge connecting them according to the similarity of the text generated by each one of the nodes. We identify several design decisions for the process.

Node vs. Edge Each edge $e_{ij} \in G$ is associated with textual content d_{ij}. We can characterize the textual content from the point of view of the *node* by aggregating the text over all its outgoing edges (i.e., $\mathbf{D}_i$), or alternatively, we can characterize the textual content from the edge point of view, by only looking at the text contained in the relevant outgoing *edges* (i.e., $\mathbf{D}_{ij}$).

Representing Textual Content using Topic Models vs. Word Embedding Before we compute the similarity between the content of two parties, we need a vector space model to represent the textual information (the set of documents $\mathbf{D}_i$, or $\mathbf{D}_{ij}$). One obvious method for this is topic modeling, in which the textual content is represented as a topic distribution. In this approach, we learn a topic model over the set of documents, and then represent each document via a set of topic weights ($\mathbf{T}_i$ or $\mathbf{T}_{ij}$). An alternative approach is using word embedding, which has been proved effective as a word representation. In this approach, we represent each document as the average of the embedding over the words in the document ($\mathbf{WE}_i$ or $\mathbf{WE}_{ij}$). Given the distributional representation of text associated with a node/edge, we assign a weight (w_{ij}) for each edge (e_{ij}) as the cosine similarity between vector representation of contents from neighboring nodes (e.g., $d(\mathbf{T}_i, \mathbf{T}_j)$ or $d(\mathbf{T}_{ij}, \mathbf{T}_{ji})$, where d is cosine similarity).

3.2 Node Embedding

We utilize the LINE embedding technique (Tang et al., 2015), aimed at preserving network structures when generating node embedding for social and information networks. LINE uses edge weights corresponding to the number of interactions between each pair of nodes. This only makes use of the network structure, without taking advantage of the text in the network. We modify the embedding procedure by using the edges weights $\mathbf{W}_{ij}$ described above (i.e., based on the cosine similarity of the text between nodes i, j) and use the LINE algorithm to compute a k-dimensional embedding of the nodes in G.

3.3 Feature Extraction

Distance-based Features Given a node pair represented by their k-dimensional node embedding, we generate features for the pair according to nine similarity measures. The nine measures used by us are Bray-Curtis distance, Canberra distance, Chebyshev distance, City Block (Manhattan) distance, Correlation distance, Cosine distance, Minkowski distance, Euclidean and squared Euclidean distance.

Additional Features Besides the distance-based features, we can also add one or more other basic features related to nodes in the network. These include the following: (1) Network: The number of interactions between two nodes, e.g. number of emails sent and received. (2) Unigram: The unigram feature vector for text sent for each node. (3) Word embedding features: The word embedding vector for text sent for each node. Again we use the average of word embedding to represent documents.

4 Experiments

Purdue Facebook Network We analyzed the public Purdue Facebook network data from March 2007 to March 2008, which includes 3 million post activities. Members can set friends as top (close) friends to get the timely notifications without a confirmation by the other. We collected 945 mutually top friend pairs for two users who set each other as top friend and 34633 one-way top friend pairs if there is only one of them set the other as top friend. The dataset will be referred as "Facebook" in this

Dataset	Embedding	$\emptyset$	N	W	WE	N+W	N+WE	N+W+WE
Facebook (F1)	no GE	49.45	77.80	75.04	75.09	81.23	79.14	79.26
	GE	53.36	78.54	75.82	75.68	82.09	79.11	78.39
	GE^N_{TM}	61.58	80.16	76.33	76.31	82.69	78.72	79.68
	GE^E_{TM}	78.36	80.51	77.51	77.51	80.23	79.82	80.38
	GE^N_{WE}	59.81	79.98	75.44	76.82	81.19	79.62	79.15
	GE^E_{WE}	80.66	82.49	81.96	81.07	83.31	82.06	**83.72**
Avocado (F1)	no GE	49.69	40.91	55.03	57.89	53.33	56.64	55.36
	GE	65.75	66.15	65.77	66.57	66.24	66.99	66.53
	GE^N_{TM}	66.66	66.65	66.49	**67.28**	66.83	67.12	66.84
	GE^E_{TM}	63.09	64.67	64.79	64.09	64.80	65.05	64.49
	GE^N_{WE}	61.33	64.51	64.60	63.83	65.46	64.67	65.39
	GE^E_{WE}	52.03	55.11	56.94	56.03	57.40	57.18	58.48

Table 1: Prediction results over the two datasets. We report the F1 score.

paper. We evaluated our method by a classification task of the two different social relationships.

Avocado Email Collection This collection consists of 279 e-mail accounts, from which we extracted the job titles and departments of 136 accounts. We divided these accounts into three groups, according to their positions in the company, namely executives, engineering department, and business department. We will refer to this dataset as "Avocado" in this paper. The task is defined as predicting whether two accounts belong to the same group. In order to make use of text signal. We will only consider account pairs that have correspondence between each other. There are 2232 positive and 1409 negative examples in this dataset.

4.1 Result

Using the features defined in the previous section, we train Logistic Regression classifier via scikit-learn in Python. We show the ten-fold cross-validation performance of our features on Facebook and Avocado datasets in Table 1. It represents the results of five different approaches to generate node embedding, and with or without adding additional features. GE is the original embedding method, the superscript N or E represent the Node or Edge, and the subscript TM or WE represent Topic Model or Word Embedding used to construct the TS-Infused graph respectively. The N, W, WE in the columns indicate the Network, Unigram and Word embedding as additional features. $\emptyset$ with no GE shows the result of random generated embedding. In this paper, we use LINE as the node embedding method, Latent Dirichlet Allocation (Blei et al., 2003) for topic modeling with ten topics and Skip-Gram for word embedding. The regularization parameters are optimized. Since the Facebook and Avocado datasets are unbalanced, we randomly downsamples the majority class to equate the size of both classes. The results show in the Table are the average scores of ten different random downsampling.

For Facebook dataset, the results of all embeddings constructed by TS-Infused social graph outperforms the original embedding GE. It shows the joint representation over linguistic information and network structure is more effective than only considering one of them independently. The results on Avocado dataset also confirm the advantage of shared representation. GE^N_{TM} significantly outperforms other text-based or network-based methods. The performance of aggregating text sent by a node is better than only looking at text on one outgoing edge, which is opposite to the results on Facebook dataset. This could be resulted from the difference between two prediction tasks. In the Facebook dataset, we try to distinguish strong and weak(er) friendship, in which case the messages they sent to each other are most indicative. While when we predict whether two persons belong to the same group inside a company, the interaction they had with their colleagues would tell us more about the community they are from.

Acknowledgments

We thank the reviewers for their insightful comments. This research is supported by NSF under contract number IIS-1149789.

References

Apoorv Agarwal, Augusto Corvalan, Jacob Jensen, and Owen Rambow. 2012. Social network analysis of alice in wonderland. In *Proceedings of the Workshop on Computational Linguistics for Literature*.

David M Blei, Andrew Y Ng, and Michael I Jordan. 2003. Latent dirichlet allocation. *the Journal of machine Learning research*, 3:993–1022.

Cristian Danescu-Niculescu-Mizil, Lillian Lee, Bo Pang, and Jon Kleinberg. 2012. Echoes of power: Language effects and power differences in social interaction. In *Proceedings of WWW*, pages 699–708.

David K Elson, Nicholas Dames, and Kathleen R McKeown. 2010. Extracting social networks from literary fiction. In *Proceedings of ACL*, pages 138–147. Association for Computational Linguistics.

Katja Filippova. 2012. User demographics and language in an implicit social network. In *Proceedings of EMNLP-CoNLL*, pages 1478–1488. Association for Computational Linguistics.

Ahmed Hassan, Amjad Abu-Jbara, and Dragomir Radev. 2012. Detecting subgroups in online discussions by modeling positive and negative relations among participants. In *Proceedings of EMNLP-CoNLL*, pages 59–70. Association for Computational Linguistics.

Vinodh Krishnan and Jacob Eisenstein. 2014. " you're mr. lebowski, i'm the dude": Inducing address term formality in signed social networks. *arXiv preprint arXiv:1411.4351*.

Ravi Kumar, Jasmine Novak, and Andrew Tomkins. 2010. Structure and evolution of online social networks. In *Link mining: models, algorithms, and applications*, pages 337–357. Springer.

Jure Leskovec, Lars Backstrom, Ravi Kumar, and Andrew Tomkins. 2008. Microscopic evolution of social networks. In *Proceedings of the 14th ACM SIGKDD international conference on Knowledge discovery and data mining*, pages 462–470. ACM.

Jure Leskovec, Daniel Huttenlocher, and Jon Kleinberg. 2010. Predicting positive and negative links in online social networks. In *Proceedings of the 19th international conference on World wide web*, pages 641–650. ACM.

Miller McPherson, Lynn Smith-Lovin, and James M Cook. 2001. Birds of a feather: Homophily in social networks. *Annual review of sociology*, pages 415–444.

Tomas Mikolov, Wen-tau Yih, and Geoffrey Zweig. 2013. Linguistic regularities in continuous space word representations. In *Proceedings of NAACL*.

Jeffrey Pennington, Richard Socher, and Christopher D. Manning. 2014. Glove: Global vectors for word representation. In *Proceedings of EMNLP*, pages 1532–1543.

Bryan Perozzi, Rami Al-Rfou, and Steven Skiena. 2014. Deepwalk: Online learning of social representations. In *Proceedings of ACM SIGKDD*, pages 701–710. ACM.

Afshin Rahimi, Duy Vu, Trevor Cohn, and Timothy Baldwin. 2015. Exploiting text and network context for geolocation of social media users.

Maarten Sap, Gregory Park, Johannes C Eichstaedt, Margaret L Kern, David Stillwell, Michal Kosinski, Lyle H Ungar, and H Andrew Schwartz. 2014. Developing age and gender predictive lexica over social media.

Jian Tang, Meng Qu, Mingzhe Wang, Ming Zhang, Jun Yan, and Qiaozhu Mei. 2015. Line: Large-scale information network embedding. In *Proceedings of WWW*, pages 1067–1077. International World Wide Web Conferences Steering Committee.

Matje Van De Camp and Antal van den Bosch. 2011. A link to the past: constructing historical social networks. In *Proceedings of the Workshop on Computational Approaches to Subjectivity and Sentiment Analysis*, pages 61–69. Association for Computational Linguistics.

Svitlana Volkova, Glen Coppersmith, and Benjamin Van Durme. 2014. Inferring user political preferences from streaming communications. In *Proceedings of ACL*, pages 186–196.

Svitlana Volkova, Yoram Bachrach, Michael Armstrong, and Vijay Sharma. 2015. Inferring latent user properties from texts published in social media.

Robert West, Hristo S Paskov, Jure Leskovec, and Christopher Potts. 2014. Exploiting social network structure for person-to-person sentiment analysis. *TACL*.

Rongjing Xiang, Jennifer Neville, and Monica Rogati. 2010. Modeling relationship strength in online social networks. In *Proceedings of the 19th international conference on World wide web*, pages 981–990. ACM.

Visualization of Dynamic Reference Graphs

Ivan Rodin and **Ekaterina Chernyak** and **Mikhail Dubov** and **Boris Mirkin**
National Research University Higher School of Economics
Moscow, Russia
ivvrodin@gmail.com

Abstract

We present a tool for dynamic reference graph visualization. A reference graph is a graph based on key phrases retrieved from a time-indexed natural language text corpus. This tool may be useful for the analysis of connected pairs of latent topics, changes in the significance of these topics as well as in the relationship between them over various time periods.

1 Introduction

"Text visualization" is a rather ambiguous term. One of the approaches to text visualization is scene generation, as described in (Chang et al., 2014). In our work, however, text visualization has a different meaning. Our interest lies in plotting meaningful elements from texts such as key phrases, named entities or terms. Retrieved plots may serve as a tool for information extraction and summarization. As shown in (Kucher and Kerren, 2015), there are many techniques for textual data analysis and visualization, and their number is rapidly growing.

In fact, the problem of text visualizaton can be divided into two subproblems: visualization of static and temporal textual data. The most known static text visualization technique is called "tag clouds" (Coupland, 1996). Many visualization techniques extend the idea of a tag cloud. For instance, in (Greene et al., 2015) key phrases are used to construct a concept lattice for a dataset of publications. Lattice is visualized as an interactive tag cloud browser. In (Coppersmith and Erin, 2014), tags extracted from tweets are colored according to the political preferences of tweet authors. Vennclouds, introduced in (Wang et al., 2012) present another extention of tags clouds, comparing two texts by showing three tag clouds: one cloud containing tags from the first text, another one with tags from second text, and the third cloud showing words and phrases that appear in both texts.

Approaches based on tag cloud construction are also quite successful in the visualization of temporal textual data. For example, the ThemeRiver visualization tool, introduced in (Havre et al., 2000), shows thematic variations over time within a large collection of documents. In (Shahaf et al., 2013), tag clouds are placed inside graph nodes. The nodes are connected by an edge if they have a lot in common, and are placed on the time axis as well.

Tag graphs are another extension of tag clouds. To construct a tag graph, one needs to introduce some sort of relation between tags. For example, in (Lloyd and D. Kechagias, 2005), the tags stand for named entities and one draws edges between tags that co-occur. (Berendt and Subasic, 2009) present a dynamic visualization technique for these temporal co-occurence graphs.

In this paper, we suggest an approach to temporal textual data analysis which is based on dynamical reference graphs. The main difference of these reference graphs from co-occurence graphs is that they are oriented. This allows to analyze how one term "refers" to another, as well as to retrieve more patterns describing the relations between terms. Our visualization also allows to analyze how the significance of certain terms changes over time.

Proceedings of the 2016 Workshop on Graph-based Methods for Natural Language Processing, NAACL-HLT 2016, pages 34–38,
San Diego, California, June 17, 2016.

2 Dynamic reference graph

To build a dynamic reference graph for a text collection, one can use Algorithm 1.

Algorithm 1: Dynamic reference graph construction

Input : Time-indexed corpus of text documents and a list of key phrases.
Output: Dynamic reference graph.

Divide the corpus evenly into T sequential time periods $\tau = 1..T$.
Set a list of N key phrases (concepts) $w_i, i = 1..N$.
for $\tau = 1..T$ **do**
    Extract the information about static weighted oriented reference graph G_τ that should include: 1) significance (the support value) of each concept in period $S_\tau(w_i)$, which is the number of documents where the concept appeared; 2) reference significance levels $C_\tau(w_i, w_j)$, $C_\tau(w_j, w_i)$ for all pairs of concepts w_i, w_j.
end
Define the lower threshold for support and confidence levels. Draw a reference graph G_1 for $\tau = 1$ with respect to these thresholds.
for $\tau = 2..T$ **do**
    Remove edges from $G_{\tau-1}$ are not in G_τ
    Remove nodes from $G_{\tau-1}$ are not in G_τ
    Add nodes from G_τ that are not in $G_{\tau-1}$
    Add edges from G_τ that are not in $G_{\tau-1}$
end

Initial steps. The input to our system is a time-indexed corpus. The system divides documents into several time periods assuming that the number of documents in each time period is commensurable.

Next, we should define a list of concepts. They can be chosen just as the top frequent terms from the corpus. Sometimes it also makes sense to set the list of concepts manually. For example, if we want to analyze some specific topics from a corpus of newspaper articles, we can set a list of keywords to monitor and analyze, for example, only economical or technological news. This approach can be also useful in the analysis of the interaction between characters in fiction books where the concepts are just their names. Other possible approaches for term extraction are presented in (Siddiqi and Sharan, 2015)

Building G_τ. Concepts define the nodes of G_τ. Weighted oriented edges of this graph are defined by the co-occurrence of these concepts. We also retrieve and store information about the significance of each concept in all time periods.

Support estimation. Let us define the significance of a concept w_i in time period τ as $S_\tau(w_i) = |D_\tau(w_i)|$, where $D_\tau(w_i)$ is a set of documents in τ where concept w_i appears more than σ times. By default, we take $\sigma = 0$, but in some cases that threshold may be increased.

Confidence estimation. Once we know the support values for each concept w_i in τ, we can compute confidence values for the connections between pairs of concepts with non-zero support values. We say that concept w_i "refers" to concept w_j in time period τ with confidence $C_\tau(w_i, w_j)$, where $C_\tau(w_i, w_j) = \frac{|D_\tau(w_i) \cap D_\tau(w_j)|}{|D_\tau(w_i)|} \in [0; 1]$.

Having computed these confidence levels for connections between concepts in time period τ, we can finally build a static oriented weighted graph G_τ for that time period. An edge from concept w_i to concept w_j with weight $C_\tau(w_i, w_j)$ in this graph means that w_i refers to w_j with confidence $C_\tau(w_i, w_j)$. We can also specify the threshold for confidence which defines wheter or not edges should be displayed. Note that values of $C_\tau(w_i, w_j)$ close to 1 mean that if w_i occurs in a document, then w_j usually occurs as well. In other words, w_j tends to occur in the context of w_i.

3 Datasets

Our test collection corresponds to the topic of newspaper analysis. We have collected a set of articles on economics from four Russian newsportals ("Izvestia", "Kommersant", "Moscow Komsomoltes", "Nezavisimaya gazeta") that were published in 2014. This corpus (called "RuNeWC" – Russian Newspaper Web Corpus) contains 4061 Russian language articles, divided into 26 time periods. Every period has a length of 2 weeks.

Concepts were extracted automatically using the strategy proposed in (Hulth, 2003), which consists of 2 steps. The first step was to extract candidate words and phrases that satisfy certain speech patterns, adopted from (Mitrofanova and Zaharov, 2009) (ex.: ADJECTIVE+NOUN, NOUN+NOUN, etc.). The next step was to form the list of concepts, which resulted in 250 most frequent phrases and 100 most frequent words. Finally, we manually removed some concepts that are not semantically important (ex.: "Kommersant reporter" ["Korrespondent Kommersanta"]). For graph visualization, we set the confidence threshold at 28 and support threshold at 0.9. An example of dynamic graph visualisation for RuNeWC is presented in fig. 1.

In order to provide an even more clear example, we created an English language corpus based on four books from a series of popular epic fantasy novels "A Song of Ice and Fire" (ASOIAF) written by George R. R. Martin. If we take the list of characters of that novel as an initial set of concepts the reference graph then shows the co-occurence of characters in the book pages, typical clusters of characters, the significance of characters, as well as the change of these parameters over the time.

The plot in the first four books develops linearly: every next chapter describes actions that occurred after the actions of a previous one. To construct our corpus, we divided each chapter into several equal parts (2–7 parts, depending on the size of that chapter). Each part was then taken to the corpus as a single document. Then, the set of all documents was divided into groups of 50 sequential documents, forming 14 time periods. We didn't take one chapter as a single time period, as the story of each chapter goes on behalf of one specific character, and he automatically becomes the most important one. In constrast, the division of each chapter into several documents increased the precision of our support and confidence estimations for the concepts from the book.

In our experiment, we set the term frequency threshold $\sigma = 1$, i.e. considered a concept to be mentioned in a document if it appeared in that document two or more times. The threshold for the support value was set at the level of 5, and minimum confidence value to 0.3.

As a result, we obtained a dynamic reference graph visualization that may serve as a schematic retelling of "Song of Ice and Fire" novel. Examples of dynamic graph visualisation for ASOIAF corpus are presented in figs. 2 to 4[1].

[1] Visualization video is available at https://youtu.be/UaUGVPTdM-w.

4 Visualization

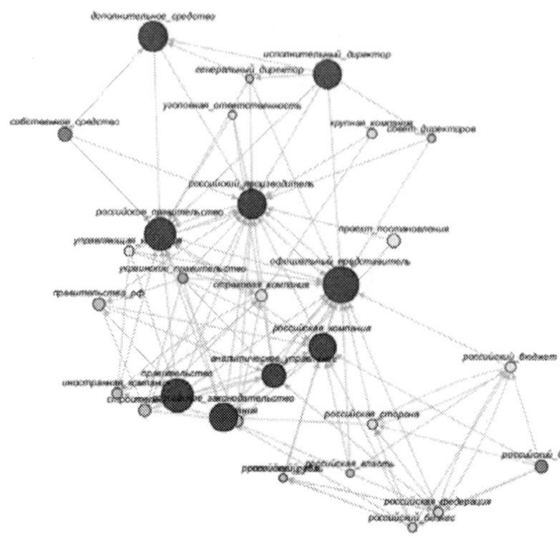

Figure 1: RuNeWC reference graph at time period $\tau = 9$ (weeks 17-18 in 2014)

There are several tools for dynamic graph visualization, such as GraphStream[2], KeyLines[3], Gephi[4]. For our task, we decided to use GraphStream as it is a well-documented Java Library which was specifically created for dynamic graphs editing and visualization. GraphStream is also effective in visualization of large graphs with thousands of nodes as it allows to create zoomable interface.

Our software tool can animate dynamic reference graphs based on their textual description. It ensures that the layout of a reference graph G_τ for time period $\tau > 1$ depends on the layout of $G_{\tau-1}$. It also takes into account the information about the support of concepts: the greater the support, the bigger the corresponding node. The "age" of concepts (number of periods where these concepts consecutively appear) is quite important as well: new nodes are marked with yellow, and when they become older, they gradually turn into blue. Moreover, if a concept appears for the first time (not after a break), the corresponding node receives a wide black border.

Our implementation comes with a graphical user interface. At any time step, the user can pause the animation process to explore the graph structure. All nodes of the input graph can be moved by simple

[2] http://graphstream-project.org/
[3] http://cambridge-intelligence.com/keylines/
[4] https://gephi.org/

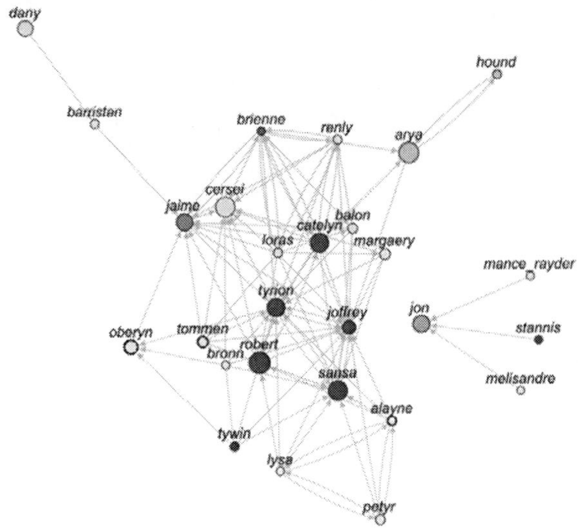

Figure 2: This is dynamic graph at time period $\tau = 11$, which corresponds to the end of the third book. Color and border differentiation of nodes can show the age of concept in graph. For ex.: Oberyn is a character that appears for the first time, as corresponding node is yellow with wide border, while "Tyrion" and other three nodes with deep blue colour have been presented in all periods from the very beginning.

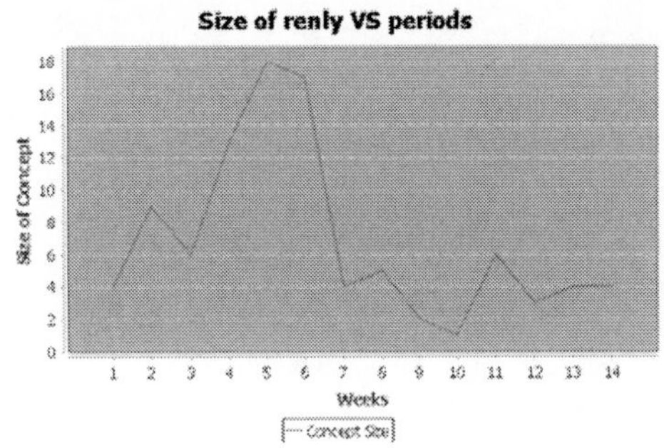

Figure 3: The change of support for concept *Renly* during the time periods.

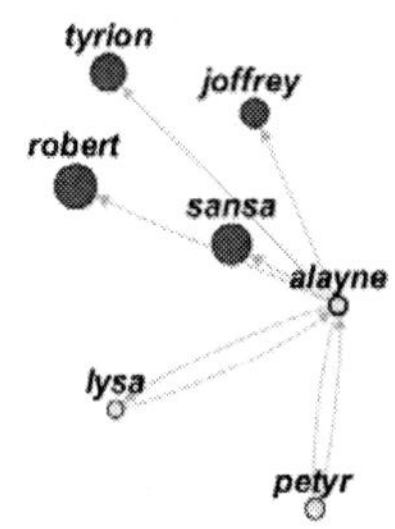

Figure 4: As node of graph is clicked only nodes connected with chosen one are displayed.

drag and drop actions. Our software also handles node clicks: once a node is clicked, only those edges and nodes that are adjacent to it are displayed. Moreover, the information about the support of the corresponding concept during all time periods is displayed in a separate window.

5 Future Work

Let us mention some future directions of our work:

Integration. We are going to integrate our visualization software with a corpus browser that will allow users to generate and visualize their own corpora. To achieve that, we will have to build a unified system that will be responsible for both graph construction and visualization. The concept extraction system will be improved as well: it is possible to use the annotated suffix tree method (Dubov, 2015) for automatic concept extraction in case the user does not provide any.

Analysis of connections. The system presented in this paper can be improved by adding support for contextual synonym extraction, as, for example, *Petyr – Lord Baelish – Littlefinger* in the ASOIAF corpus or *Russian president – Vladimir Putin* in the RuNeWC corpus. We will also compare presented mesure for confidence estimation with other similarity measures.

Graph analysis. Temporal cluster analysis can be particularly informative. Retrieving and highlighting of strongly connected components would allow users to detect some strong ongoing trends.

Graph layout. The layout of dynamic graphs still can be improved. In particular, we have to solve the problem of overlapping nodes that occasionally appears in our software.

Acknowledgements

We would like to express our sincere gratitude to Dmitry Ilvovsky, Anna Shishkova and Maxim Yakovlev, members of research and study group "Methods of web corpus texts analysis and visualisation" for their large contribution to this work. This study (research grant No 15-05-0041) was supported by The National Research University Higher School of Economics Academic Fund Program in 2015.

References

B. Berendt and I. Subasic. 2009. *Stories in time: A graphbased interface for news tracking and discovery.* In WI-IAT09.

A. X. Chang, M. Savva, and C. D Manning. 2014. *Semantic parsing for text to 3d scene generation.* In Proceedings of the ACL 2014 Workshop on Semantic Parsing.

G. Coppersmith and K. Erin. 2014. *Dynamic Wordclouds and Vennclouds for Exploratory Data Analysis.* Association for Computational Linguistics.

D. Coupland. 1996. Microserfs, Flamingo.

Mikhail Dubov. 2015. Text analysis with enhanced annotated suffix trees: Algorithms and implementation. In *Analysis of Images, Social Networks and Texts - 4th International Conference, AIST 2015, Yekaterinburg, Russia, April 9-11, 2015, Revised Selected Papers*, pages 308–319.

Gillian J Greene, Marcel Dunaiski, Bernd Fischer, Dmitry Ilvovsky, and Sergei O Kuznetsov. 2015. Browsing publication data using tag clouds over concept lattices constructed by key-phrase extraction.

Susan Havre, Beth Hetzler, and Lucy Nowell. 2000. *ThemeRiver: Visualizing Theme Changes over Time.* Proceedings of the IEEE Symposium on Information Vizualization 2000.

A. Hulth. 2003. *Improved automatic keyword extraction given more linguistic knowledge.* The conference on Empirical methods in natural language processing.

K. Kucher and A. Kerren. 2015. *Text visualization browser: A visual survey of text visualization techniques.* Proceedings of IEEE Pacific Visualization Symposium (Visualization Notes), Englewood Cliffs, NJ.

L. Lloyd and S. Skiena D. Kechagias. 2005. *Lydia: A system for large-scale news analysis, String Processing and Information Retrieval.* Springer Berlin Heidelberg.

O. A. Mitrofanova and V. P. Zaharov. 2009. *Automatic Analysis of Terminology in the Russian Text Corpus on Corpus Linguistics [Avtomatizirovannyy analiz terminologii v russkoyazyichnom korpuse tekstov po korpusnoy lingvistike],.* Dialog, available at: http://www.dialog-21.ru/digests/dialog2009/materials/.

Dafna Shahaf, Jaewon Yang, Caroline Suen, Heidi Wang Jeff Jacobs, and Jure Leskovec. 2013. *Information cartography: creating zoomable, large-scale maps of information.* Proceedings of the 19th ACM SIGKDD international conference on Knowledge discovery and data mining.

S. Siddiqi and A. Sharan. 2015. Keyword and keyphrase extraction techniques: A literature review. *International Journal of Computer Applications*, 109(2).

H. Wang, D. Can, A. Kazemzadeh, F. Bar, and S. Narayanan. 2012. *A system for realtime twitter sentiment analysis of 2012 US presidential election cycle.* Proceedings of the ACL 2012 System Demonstrations. Association for Computational Linguistics.

Association for Computational Linguistics
209 N. Eighth Street
Stroudsburg, Pennsylvania 18360

ISBN 978-1-5108-2516-1

CURRAN ASSOCIATES INC.
proceedings.com